BRIGHT SKIES AHEAD

BRIGHT SKIES AHEAD:
Overcoming Life's Storms

ADENIJI RAJI, mni

Readers' Testimonials

A heartwarming and inspiring book that reminds us we're never alone in our struggles."
— ***Olutayo Irantiola***

"A must-read for anyone seeking hope and positivity during tough times."
— ***Tunji Funsho***

Copyright © 2024 by Adeniji Raji.

All rights reserved.

No part of this book may be reproduced or transmitted in any form by any means, electronic or mechanical, including photocopying and recording, or by any information storage and retrieval system, except as may be expressly permitted in writing from the author.

Printed in the United States of America

Dedication

*Dedicated to every heart that has weathered a storm and emerged stronger.
May your journey be filled with hope and brighter skies.*

Preface

As I began writing "Bright Skies Ahead: Overcoming Life's Storms," I reflected on the many moments in my life. The uncertainty, the pain, the fear—it felt like the storms would never end. Each time, I found a way to navigate through the turmoil, discovering new strengths, learning valuable lessons.

In life, we are all travelers on a tumultuous journey, navigating through the highs and lows, the joys and sorrows that shape our paths. "Bright Skies Ahead: Overcoming Life's Storms" is a heartfelt exploration of the trials and tribulations that we face along the way.

As the author of this book, I have walked through the valleys of despair and scaled the mountains of hope. I have weathered the storms that threatened to drown me and basked in the sunlight that followed. Through it all, I have learned that life's challenges are not meant to break us but to mold us into the individuals we are destined to become.

This book is a collection of stories, insights, and strategies designed to help others who face similar challenges. It's not about my journey; it's about all us and the resilience we find when life throws its most daunting storms our way. The stories within these pages come from people of various backgrounds, each with their unique experiences and ways of coping. These narratives aim to inspire and show that no matter how dark the clouds, there is always a break in the storm.

I've been fortunate to have the support of friends, family, and professionals who believed in this project. They understood that the journey wasn't always easy, but they encouraged me to keep going. To them, I am grateful.

"Bright Skies Ahead" is not a definitive guide to overcoming every challenge. Instead, it's a collection of tools, thoughts, and encouragement meant to serve as a companion during difficult times. I hope it becomes a source of comfort and guidance for you, the reader, as you navigate through your own storms.

As you turn the pages, I invite you to explore, reflect, and find some light in the midst of your struggles. It's my sincere wish that this book helps you discover the strength within yourself and the support from those around you. If you find even a glimmer of hope here, then this journey has been worthwhile.

Thank you for joining me on this path. that together, we can weather any storm and find brighter skies ahead.

Acknowledgments

Writing a book is a journey that requires support, encouragement, and guidance from many people. I am grateful to everyone who contributed to "Bright Skies Ahead: Overcoming Life's Storms." This book is a testament to the collaborative efforts of those who believed in its message and helped bring it to life.

To my family, thank you for your unwavering support and patience. Your encouragement during the long nights and early mornings spent writing kept me going. Your love and understanding have been my rock through every storm.

To my friends, you have been my sounding boards, my cheerleaders, and my motivators. Whether it was brainstorming ideas or providing constructive feedback, you played a crucial role in shaping this book. I cherish your insights and the laughter we shared along the way.

To my mentors, thank you for guiding me through the process of writing and publishing. Your wisdom and expertise have been invaluable. You inspired me to embrace the challenges and persevere with courage.

I thank the individuals who shared their personal stories and experiences in this book, thank you for your bravery and openness. Your willingness to share your journeys is what makes this book a source of inspiration and hope for others.

I would like to acknowledge the invaluable contributions of Google and artificial intelligence, which have greatly enhanced my research and enriched the insights presented in this book.

Finally, to the readers—thank you for picking up this book. I hope it serves as a beacon of light during challenging times. My deepest desire is that you find strength, comfort, and motivation in its pages. If this book helps you navigate through life's storms or brings you a sense of hope, then every effort was worth it.

Thank you all for being a part of this journey. Your support has made all the difference.

Contents

Preface .... **ix**
Acknowledgments .... **xi**
Introduction: Purpose of the Book **1**
Personal Anecdote **3**

Chapter 1: Understanding the Storms **5**
    1.1 Defining Challenges 5
    1.2 Common Reactions 6
    1.3 Recognizing these Emotions. 6
    1.4 Navigating the Challenges 7
    1.5 Navigating Life's Storms with Resilience ? .. 10
    1.6 Mental Health and Resilience 46

Chapter 2: Preparing for the Storms **49**
    2.1 How to Survive Adversity 49
    2.2. Cultivate a Positive Mindset 50
    2.3. Develop Strong Relationships 50
    2.4. Emotional Regulation Techniques 50
    2.5 Adaptability and Flexibility 55
    2.6. Physical Self-Care 55
    2.7 . Problem-Solving Skills 56
    2.8. Purpose and Meaning 56
    2.9. Stress Management Techniques 57
    2.10. Self-Compassion 57
    2.11. Professional Support and Learning 57
    2.12 Meditation to Improve Your Mental Health . 58

2.13 Setting Goals · 62
2.14 Emotional Preparedness · 64
2.15 Strengthening Social Networks · · · · · · · · · · · · · · · · · 64

Chapter 3: Navigating Through the Storm · · · · · · · · · · · · · · · 75
3.1 Understanding the Storm · 75
3.2 Taking Control of What You Can · · · · · · · · · · · · · · · · · 75
3.3 Mindset Shifts: Concepts for Embracing Change and Building Resilience · 83
3.4 Tools and Strategies for Navigating Life's Challenges · · · · · · · · 85
3.5 Learning from Real-Life Stories · · · · · · · · · · · · · · · · · · 88
3.6 Key Lessons: Strategies for Navigating Through Life's Storms · · 91
3.7 Personal Anecdotes : Finding Support During Challenging Times 94

Chapter 4: Embracing Change—Exploring the Concept of Change and Growth During Difficult Times · · · · · · · 97
4.1 The Nature · 97
4.2 Strategies for Embracing Change · · · · · · · · · · · · · · · · · 98
4.3 Strategies for Embracing Change and Finding Opportunities for Growth · 103
4.4 Adapting and Evolving in the face of Adversity · · · · · · · · · · · 107

Chapter 5: After the Rain—Finding Hope and Growth Beyond the Storm · 111
5.1 The Aftermath of the Storm · 111
5.2 Post-Traumatic Growth · 112
5.3 Embracing Change and New Beginnings · · · · · · · · · · · · · · 114
5.4 Moving Forward with Purpose · · · · · · · · · · · · · · · · · · · 115
5.5 Practicing Gratitude and Mindfulness · · · · · · · · · · · · · · · 115
5.6 Post-Adversity Growth: Transforming Challenges into Opportunities · 116
5.7 Strategies for Fostering Post-Adversity Growth · · · · · · · · · · · 119

5.8 Personal Stories of Finding Hope and Optimism in the Midst of Adversity** · 120
5.9 Moving Forward: Embracing the Path Ahead After Adversity** · 123
5.10 Encouragement to Keep Pushing Forward and Never Give Up · 125

Chapter 6: THE SKY IS THE LIMIT · **131**
6.1 Embracing Infinite Possibilities · 131
6.2 Setting New Goals: Encouraging Readers to Aim Higher · · · · · · 132
6.3 Continuous Growth: The Importance of Lifelong Learning and Development · 135

Chapter 7: Empowering Others · **141**
7.1 The Ripple Effect of Empowerment · 141
7.2 The Art of Active Listening · 142
7.3 Offering Practical Support · 142
7.4 Inspiring Through Example · 143
7.5 Celebrating the Success of Others · 143
7.6 Conclusion: A Call to Action · 143

Chapter 8: The Gift of Adversity · **145**
8.1 Embracing the Storm · 145
8.2 Lessons in Resilience · 146
8.3 Finding Silver Linings · 146
8.4 The Transformative Power of Perspective · · · · · · · · · · · · · · · · 146
8.5 Conclusion: A Tribute to Strength · 147

Chapter 9: The Dawn of Hope · **149**
9.1 Embracing the Journey · 149
9.2 Cultivating a Mindset of Hope · 150
9.3 The Strength of Community · 150
9.4 The Power of Resilience · 151
9.5 A Call to Keep Moving Forward · 151
9.6 Conclusion: Hope is Always Ahead · 151

Chapter 10: Recap of Key Themes and Takeaways from "Bright Skies Ahead: Overcoming Life's Storms" · 153
    10.1 Understanding the Storms · 153
    10.2 Preparing for the Storms · 153
    10.3 Navigating Through the Storms · 154
    10.4 Embracing Change and Growth · 154
    10.5 After the Rain · 154
    10.6 The Sky is the Limit · 154
    10.7 Empowering Others · 154
    10.8 The Gift Of Adversity · 155
    10.9 The Dawn of Hope · 155

Chapter 11: Final Thoughts · 157
    11.1 Encouragement to Embrace the Journey of Overcoming Life's Storms · 157
    11.2 Message of Hope and Positivity for the Future · 159

APPENDICES · 163
    Appendix A: Coping Tools and Techniques · 163
    Appendix B: Resources for Mental Health and Support · 175
    Appendix C: Goal Setting and Tracking Templates · 177
    Appendix D: Inspirational Quotes and Affirmations · 178
    Appendix E: Recommended Books and Articles · 181
    Appendix F: Worksheets for Reflection and Growth · 182
    Appendix G: Relationship Building and Communication · 191
    Appendix H: Recommended References for Further Reading · 192

Introduction: Purpose of the Book

Welcome to "Bright Skies Ahead: Overcoming Life's Storms." This book is a journey, a guide, and a companion for those who are facing the tumultuous weathers of life. The book offers you solace, strength, and strategies to not survive but thrive.

The core aim of "Bright Skies Ahead" is to help you find the light even during the darkest times. It's about transforming the way you perceive and handle life's inevitable challenges. Yet, it is often in our darkest times that we can find our brightest light—our resilience.

In the coming chapters, you will discover insights into understanding the nature of your challenges. This book is not about coping with adversity; it's about moving beyond it to a place where you can look back and see how far you've come, how much you've grown.

I invite you to use this book as a toolkit, a source of comfort, and a beacon of hope. You will not only have navigated through your current challenges but it will also equip you with courage and confidence. Let's embark on this transformative journey together, towards brighter skies and new horizons.

Personal Anecdote

Many years ago, I found myself in the middle of what felt like an unending storm. It began with the sudden loss of my father when I was in High school, this spiraled into a period of deep emotional turmoil. The compounded stress felt insurmountable, and there were days I doubted my ability to see through the darkness.

One particularly difficult day, I took a walk in a nearby school playground seeking a brief escape from the weight of my troubles. It was there, watching a group of children playing carefree under the sun, that I experienced a profound realization. There can be undercurrents of pain, and, in the depths of despair, there can be glimpses of hope.

This moment was a turning point for me. I began to see my challenges not as barriers to my happiness, but as opportunities to grow and learn about myself and the world around me.

This personal journey—marked by both its lows and its highs—is what inspired me to write "Bright Skies Ahead." It is my hope that by sharing my story, you too will find the strength to move through your storms and into brighter days. Also the stories and strategies within these pages will inspire you to overcome your challenges.

CHAPTER 1:
Understanding the Storms

In life, as in nature, storms are inevitable. They come in various forms and intensities—some we see coming, while others strike without warning. Understanding these storms is the first step toward navigating through them. This chapter will help you identify the kinds of challenges you may face and recognize the common reactions that go with them.

1.1 Defining Challenges

Life's storms have four main categories:

1.1.1. Emotional challenges may arise from personal losses, relationship issues, or significant life changes.

1.1.2. Health-related issues, like sudden accidents or illnesses, fall into this category. These challenges often need not be physical healing but also emotional resilience.

1.1.3. Financial Challenges: Economic difficulties can create significant stress. Job loss, unexpected expenses, or long-term financial planning issues are common types .

1.1.4. Difficulties in relationships can have profound impacts on our mental well-being.

1.2 Common Reactions

Facing any of these storms can evoke a range of reactions. Here are some of the most typical:

1.2.1 Fear

It's natural to feel afraid when faced with uncertainty or potential loss. Fear can be both a protective response and a barrier.

1.2.2 Denial

Sometimes, our first reaction to unexpected bad news is denial. It is a defense mechanism that can give us time to adjust to a new reality.

1.2.3 Anger

Feeling angry is a common response, especially if the situation feels unfair or beyond our control.

Recognizing these reactions in ourselves can be the first step in managing them. It's important to understand that these emotions are normal responses to the challenges we face. By acknowledging them, we can begin to take control of how we respond to and manage our difficulties.

1.3 Recognizing these Emotions.

Understanding that challenges are a natural part of life helps us to prepare for them, both mentally and physically . Each type of challenge brings its own set of obstacles, but the underlying thread is their inevitability. This chapter sets the stage for learning how to equip ourselves with the right tools and mindsets. By doing so, we can transform our approach to life's storms from one of fear and avoidance to one of courage, growth, and resilience.

1.3.1 Defining Challenges:

1.3.1.1 Emotional Challenges
Emotional Challenges and How to Overcome Them

These can include:

Grief: Arising from the loss of a loved one, the end of a significant relationship, or even the loss of a job or a home.

1.3.1.2 Anxiety and Stress:
The feeling of sadness or loss of interest affects how you feel, think, and handle daily activities.

1.4 Navigating the Challenges

1.4.1 Emotional challenges
Navigating emotional challenges can be difficult, but here are some strategies that can help you manage and overcome them:

1.4.1.1 Seek Professional Help if Needed

- If your emotions feel overwhelming and are interfering with your daily life, consider seeking help from a mental health professional. Therapy can provide tools and insights to help you navigate challenging emotions.

Remember, emotional challenges are a part of life, and it's okay to ask for help when needed.

1.4.1.2 Give yourself time to heal emotionally. It's normal for progress to be slow, and practicing self-compassion is important during tough times.

These strategies can help you cope with emotional challenges more effectively and build resilience over time.

1.4.2 Physical Challenges
Physical challenges relate to our health and can affect our quality of life.

They include:

Acute Conditions: Such as injuries or sudden illnesses that need immediate attention.

Long-Term Health Issues: health problems that cant be cured but can be managed.

Disability: Physical or cognitive disabilities that impact daily functioning and personal independence.

Addressing physical challenges often involves medical intervention, lifestyle adjustments, and rehabilitation processes. Mental Health and the Importance of Community Support play a major role in this intervention.

1.4.3 Financial Challenges :
Financial issues can cause significant stress and anxiety, impacting all other areas of life.

Common financial challenges include:
Loss of Income: Due to job loss or inability to work because of physical or mental health issues.

Unexpected Expenses: Such as medical bills, home repairs, or other emergency costs.

Debt: Managing high levels of debt or navigating the complexities of bankruptcy. Financial difficulties can arise from Budgeting issues and can be resolved as follows:

1. Budgeting Issues:

- Challenge: Difficulty sticking to a budget or unexpected expenses disrupting financial plans.

- Solution: Use the 50/30/20 rule (50% needs, 30% wants, 20% savings/debt) or adopt a zero-based budget to track every dollar. Set up an emergency fund to handle unexpected expenses.

2. Insufficient Savings:

- Challenge: Lack of savings for emergencies, retirement, or future goals.

- Challenge: Impulsive purchases or living beyond means.

Financial literacy, budgeting, emergency planning, and financial advice can help manage and overcome common financial difficulties,

1.4.3 Relational Challenges
Relationships, while often a source of joy and support, can also be a source of significant emotional distress when they face problems. These challenges include:

Interpersonal Conflicts:
With family, friends, or coworkers, which can lead to stress and anxiety.

Family Divorce: can lead to increased anxiety, depression, loneliness and decreased self-esteem.

Social Isolation: Feeling disconnected from others can lead to loneliness and depression.

Effective communication, counseling, and sometimes mediation are essential tools for navigating relational challenges.

Conclusion
By defining these challenges, we not only understand their nature but also their potential impact on our lives. The Importance of a clear vision

with each type of challenge, there are approaches that one can use to each type of challenge, there are also other approaches to manage and move beyond them.

1.5 Navigating Life's Storms with Resilience ?

1.5.1 Fear
Fear is one of the most immediate reactions to any threat or challenge. It serves as a protective mechanism that alerts us to danger and prepares us to deal with it. When fear becomes overwhelming, it can paralyze us, preventing effective action and problem-solving

1.5.1.1 Fear Management
Fear is a powerful emotion that can impact our ability to handle life's challenges. When fear is managed well, it serves as a protective and motivating force; when it's not, it can become debilitating.

1.5.1.2 How to Overcome Fear
Recognizing and Acknowledging Fear

The first step in managing fear is to recognize and acknowledge it. This involves: Self-awareness: Paying attention to what triggers your fear and how it manifests in your body and behavior.

Accepting that feeling afraid is normal.

1.5.1.3 Grounding Techniques
When fear feels overwhelming, grounding techniques can help you stay in the present moment.

1.5.1.4 Breathing Exercises
Slow, deep breathing can help calm the nervous system and reduce the physical symptoms of fear.

Practicing mindfulness can help you stay connected to the present

You can apply Techniques such as focusing on tactile sensations to divert attention from fearful thoughts(Fear can reduce tactile sensitivity or ability to sense touch because fear affects the peripheral nervous system)

1.5.1.5 Cognitive-Behavioral Strategies
Cognitive-behavioral strategies involve changing the thought patterns that fuel fear:

Identify Irrational Beliefs: these include,Catastrophizing-believing that the situation is much than it is or Personalization-taking everything personally.

Challenge and reframe negative thoughts will help reduce fear.

1.5.1.6 How to Use Positive Affirmations
Using positive affirmations effectively involves creating meaningful statements that challenge negative thoughts and reinforce a positive mindset.

It is important to use affirmations consistently over time. Positive change doesn't happen overnight, but with regular practice, they can reshape thought patterns and boost self-esteem.

By using positive affirmations regularly and intentionally, you can build a more optimistic and empowered mindset.

1.5.1.7 Exposure Therapy
exposing yourself to the source of your fear in a controlled and safe manner can reduce the power that fear holds over you:

Start with less frightening aspects of the fear source and work your way up to more challenging exposures.

Virtual reality (computer -generated environment) can provide a safe environment for exposure

1.5.1.8 Building a Support Network
The Importance of a Support Network

A support network is a group of people who provide emotional, social, or practical help during times of need. It can include family, friends, colleagues, or professionals. Here are some key reasons why a support network is important:

1. Having people to share feelings with during tough times provides a sense of belonging and comfort.

2. Support networks can help you see issues from different angles and provide practical advice or solutions.

3. Support Networks improves your self-esteem

4. Support Networks help you stay focused and resilient

5. Strong Support Networks lead to better mental health.

6. Knowing that there are people you can count on makes it easier to recover from setbacks and maintain mental strength.

In summary, having a support network fosters emotional well-being, personal growth, and resilience. It creates a safety net that helps you navigate the ups and downs of life.

1.5.1.9 Friends and Family:
Sharing your fears with trusted people can help you feel less alone and more understood.

Therapists or counselors can provide guidance and strategies tailored to your specific needs.

1.5.1.10 Lifestyle Adjustments
Maintaining a healthy lifestyle can enhance your emotional resilience:

How to Reduce Fear and Anxiety Levels

- Adequate Sleep:
  A well-rested mind is better equipped to handle emotional stress, including fear.

- Balanced Diet:
  Proper nutrition can affect your mood and energy levels, influencing how you handle fear.

Conclusion
By employing these strategies, you can start to take back control from fear. Remember, the goal isn't to end fear but to manage it so that it doesn't hinder your ability to face life's challenges. As you become more adept at managing fear, you'll find that you can approach difficult situations with a clearer mind and a stronger sense of purpose.

1.5.2 Denial
Denial is a defense mechanism that helps cushion the shock of a distressing situation. It involves refusing to accept the reality of a painful event, which can give us time to adjust.

Examples:
Denying the severity of a financial crisis or ignoring symptoms of a chronic illness.

1.5.2.1 Denial Management Strategies
Gradual acceptance is key.

Denial is a common initial reaction to unpleasant situations or distressing information. But, prolonged denial can prevent effective coping and problem-solving.

1.5.2.2 Moving Beyond Denial and
Recognizing Signs of Denial

The first step in overcoming denial is to recognize its signs, which might include:

- Avoidance:
  Avoiding discussion or thought about a distressing topic.

- Minimization:
  Downplaying the severity or consequences of the situation.

- Rationalization:
  Offering unreasonable excuses for the situation or one's behavior.

1.5.2.3 Gentle Confrontation
It's important to confront denial without overwhelming yourself or others. You can archieve this through:

- Self-reflection:
  Taking time to reflect on your thoughts and feelings can help you identify areas where you might be in denial.

1.5.2.4 What to do if you're a CEO or a CTO?
Denial, in a business context, can be a dangerous mindset for leaders, especially for those in key positions like a CEO or CTO. Denial can prevent you from seeing potential risks, market changes, or internal issues. Here's what you can do if you find yourself or your team slipping into denial:

1. Acknowledge the Issue

- The first step to overcoming denial is recognizing it. Be honest with yourself about the state of the business. If problems exist—be it financial instability, a technological bottleneck, or a changing market—acknowledge them.

- Encourage feedback from your team and create an environment where they feel safe pointing out issues without fear of repercussions.

2. Seek External Perspectives

- Sometimes, it's hard to see issues from within. Bringing in external consultants, advisors, or mentors can help provide fresh perspectives on challenges the company is facing.

- engage with industry peers, analysts, or stakeholders to get an outsider's view of the business landscape and your position in it.

3. Use Data to Drive Decisions

- Relying on data can help combat denial. Ensure decisions are made based on hard facts, not gut feelings or wishful thinking. Implement dashboards and KPIs that give a clear, objective picture of the business's performance.

- Review key metrics such as financials, customer satisfaction, product usage, and technological performance to stay grounded in reality.

4. Foster Open Communication

- As a leader, ensure that communication channels are open across the company. Regular all-hands meetings, internal surveys, or anonymous feedback systems can help surface hidden issues or employee concerns.

- Ensure that your leadership team is aligned, and that they feel empowered to challenge assumptions and contribute ideas without fear of being shut down.

5. Create a Culture of Accountability

- Encourage accountability at all levels of the organization. Leaders must set an example by taking responsibility when things go wrong and by learning from mistakes.

- Cultivate a culture where performance is evaluated, and where both successes and failures are discussed.

6. Be Willing to Pivot

- In times of denial, many leaders hold onto a failing strategy, unwilling to pivot due to the investment already made. It's crucial to know when to shift direction, even if it means abandoning a project or rethinking a core product.

- Stay adaptable preparedto make difficult decisions, such as changing product direction, restructuring teams, or reallocating resources.

7. Encourage Innovation and Experimentation

- Often, denial is rooted in an unwillingness to change or innovate. Encourage experimentation within your teams, and be willing to test new ideas, even if they challenge the status quo.

- Allocate time and resources for research and development to keep your organization ahead of industry trends and technological advancements.

8. Engage with Customers and the Market

- seek feedback from customers and pay attention to market trends. Understanding customer pain points or shifts in the competitive landscape can help you avoid being blindsided.

- Be open to changing customer needs and adjust your product or service offerings.

9. Embrace Humility

- As a leader, it's important to accept that you don't have all the answers. Recognizing the limits of your own knowledge or assumptions is crucial in overcoming denial.

- Show humility by listening to others, admitting mistakes, and being open to learning from both successes and failures.

10. Address Internal Conflicts and Biases

- Denial can sometimes stem from internal biases or conflicts within the leadership team. Addressing these head-on can help ensure that everyone is aligned and that decisions are made in the best interest of the company, not individual egos.

- Seek to identify and reduce any cognitive biases such as confirmation bias or groupthink, which can lead to denial and poor decision-making.

By staying vigilant, data-driven, and open to change, a CEO or CTO can confront denial and ensure their organization remains adaptable and responsive to challenge

1.5.2.5 Education and Information Gathering
Understanding the reality of the situation can help break through denial:

- Identifying and addressing the problem in a real-world problem

- The Importance of Professional Guidance

- Incremental Acceptance
  Accepting reality can be a gradual process, especially if the situation is particularly painful or life-changing:

- Small Steps:
  Begin by acknowledging small aspects of the situation before addressing the whole.

- Emotional Support
  Having a supportive network is crucial in moving past denial:

1.5.2.6 Isolation: Keeping Fiends
Identifying and Keeping Friends

Identifying and keeping friends requires intentional effort, understanding, and nurturing relationships over time. Building meaningful friendships is about finding people who share similar values, interests, and who provide mutual support. Below are steps to help you identify and maintain strong, lasting friendships:

How to Identify Friends

A. Look for Common Interests

- Shared Hobbies: Engage in activities you enjoy, such as sports, art, volunteering, or clubs. This connects you with people who have similar interests.

Join groups that focus on your passions, such as book clubs, sports teams, or hobbyist communities. This creates opportunities to meet like-minded people.

B. Find People with Shared Values
People who share similar values are more likely to foster genuine and lasting friendships.

- Seek Mutual Respect: Look for people who treat you with respect, appreciate your boundaries, and value your opinions. This mutual respect is key to healthy friendships.

C. Observe Their Behavior

- Reliability: A good friend is dependable and follows through on promises. If someone shows up for you, they're worth investing time in.

- Supportiveness: Look for friends who encourage you in tough times and celebrate your successes. Positive energy is a strong indicator of a healthy friendship.

- Good Communication: Friends should listen to you without judgment and be willing to communicate and. This forms the foundation of strong relationships.

D. Assess Compatibility

- Energy Levels: Some people are more introverted, while others are extroverted. Find friends whose energy levels and social needs align with your own to avoid mismatches.

2. How to Keep Friends

A. Communicate

- Stay in Touch: Regular communication is key to maintaining friendships. Make an effort to check in, send messages, or plan calls, even if it's to say hello.

- Active Listening: When interacting, practice active listening. Give them your full attention, acknowledge their feelings, and show genuine interest in their thoughts.

B. Be Supportive

- Emotional Support: Be there for your friends during tough times. Offer a listening ear, encouragement, or even practical help when they need it.

- Celebrate Successes: Don't be present in hard times.

C. Respect Boundaries

- Give Space: Understand that friends have different needs, and sometimes they may need space or time for themselves. Respect their boundaries without taking it.

- Don't Overwhelm: Friendships thrive when both parties respect each other's limits. Avoid being too demanding or clingy; allow the relationship to grow.

D. Be Honest and Trustworthy

- Share: Build trust by being open and honest with your friends. Share your thoughts and feelings in a respectful way, and encourage them to do the same.

- Be Loyal: Trust is crucial in friendships. Don't gossip about or betray a friend's confidence. Be someone they can rely on for discretion and support.

E. Show Appreciation

- Express Gratitude: let your friends know that you value and appreciate them. A simple thank-you, compliment, or thoughtful gesture can go a long way in reinforcing bonds.

- Make Time for Them: Show that you value the friendship by prioritizing time to spend with them, whether it's in person or.

F. Resolve Conflicts

- Address Issues: Conflicts may arise in friendships, but it's important to address them in a calm, respectful manner. Talk about any issues without blaming or accusing.

- Apologize When Needed: If you make a mistake, don't hesitate to apologize. Taking responsibility for your actions helps mend and strengthen the friendship.

- Forgive and Move Forward: If your friend acknowledges their mistake and apologizes, try to forgive them and move forward. Holding onto grudges can damage the relationship.

G. Make Effort in Maintaining Friendship

- Be Present: Be there for your friend in significant moments, such as birthdays, achievements, or difficult times.

- Be Proactive: Don't wait for your friend to start plans. Take the initiative to suggest outings or catch-up sessions. Showing you care by putting in effort keeps the friendship alive.

3. Qualities of a Good Friend

- Empathy:
A good friend is understanding and empathetic. They can relate to your feelings and provide emotional support when needed.

- Trustworthiness:
Trust is the foundation of a solid friendship. You should be able to confide in your friend without fear of judgment or betrayal.

- Mutual Respect:
Healthy friendships are built on mutual respect. Both friends should appreciate each other's values, boundaries, and individuality.

- Reliability:
Good friends are dependable. You can count on them to be there when they say they will, whether it's to lend an ear or offer help.

- Fun and Joy:
  Friendships should bring joy, fun, and laughter. Being able to share positive experiences and light-hearted moments strengthens the bond.

4. Signs of a Toxic Friendship
It's important to recognize signs of unhealthy friendships and distance yourself if needed:

- Constant Criticism or Negativity: If a friend puts you down or is negative, the friendship can become draining.

- Lack of Support: If the relationship feels one-sided or your friend is never there when you need them, it's a sign of an imbalanced friendship.

- Manipulation or Control: A toxic friend may try to control you or manipulate situations to their advantage, which can be damaging.

Conclusion
To identify and keep friends, seek out those who share your values, interests, and who are emotionally supportive. Nurture the friendship by staying in touch, offering support, respecting boundaries, and resolving conflicts maturely. Ultimately, a good friendship is built on mutual trust, respect, and genuine care for each other's well-being.

1.5.2.7 How to Accept Your Denial
Setting Realistic Goals

Once you begin to move past denial, setting small, achievable goals can help you take active steps toward dealing with the situation:

Actionable Steps:

- Break down large challenges into smaller, manageable tasks.

- Regular Reviews:
  assess your progress to adapt your goals as needed.

- Practicing Self-Compassion
  Finally, it's essential to practice self-compassion throughout the process:

- Self-Talk: Mindfulness and Relaxation Techniques. Engage in practices that promote relaxation and presence.

Conclusion
By employing these strategies, you can reduce your reliance on denial as a coping mechanism.

1.5.2.8 Denial Management Strategies
Denial is a common initial reaction to unpleasant situations or distressing information. Yet, prolonged denial can prevent effective coping and problem-solving.

1.5.2.8 More Ways to Move Beyond Denial
Self-reflection: Taking time to reflect on your thoughts and feelings can help you identify areas where you might be in denial.

What to do if you're a CEO or a CTO
Self-reflection is a critical practice for anyone in a leadership role, such as a CEO or CTO. It allows you to test your decisions, leadership style, and the direction of your company or team. Regular self-reflection can help you grow and, enabling you to make better decisions and lead more. Here's a guide to self-reflection for CEOs and CTOs:

1. Assess Your Leadership Style
Key Questions:

- How do I communicate with my team? Am I approachable and clear?

- Do I empower my team or tend to micromanage?

- How do I handle feedback or dissenting opinions from my team?

- Am I leading by example omit work ethic, transparency, and accountability?

- Action: Consider asking your leadership team for 360-degree feedback. Be open to hearing how your style may be affecting team dynamics and morale, and take steps to adjust if necessary.

2. Check Decision-Making
Key Questions:

- Do I base my decisions on data, intuition, or a combination of both?

- How often do I make decisions based on assumptions, without exploring other perspectives?

- Have my recent decisions improved the company's performance or team productivity?

- Am I making decisions that align with the long-term vision of the company, or am I being reactive?

- Action: Reflect on a few recent critical decisions and check their outcomes. Were they well-informed? If not, what could you have done? question your assumptions to avoid cognitive biases.

3. Reflect on Company Vision and Strategy
Key Questions:

- Is the company moving in the right direction according to its mission and vision?

- Am I inspiring others with the company's vision, and is everyone aligned with it?

- Are we innovating enough to stay competitive, or are we stuck in our ways?

- Action: Compare the company's current trajectory with its long-term goals. Identify areas where the vision or strategy may need refining. Involve your team in discussions about the future direction to ensure alignment.

4. Understand Your Impact on Company Culture
Key Questions:

- What kind of culture am I fostering? Is it open, innovative, and inclusive, or is it rigid and hierarchical?

- How do I react to mistakes—do I encourage learning or foster fear of failure?

- Am I nurturing a work-life balance, or am I contributing to burnout?

- Action: Reflect on how your behaviors and actions influence the company culture. Make conscious efforts to create a positive, growth-oriented environment. Consider how your presence shapes the company's emotional climate.

5. Balance Short-Term and Long-Term Thinking
Key Questions:

- Am I focused on immediate results, or am I also thinking about the long-term growth and sustainability of the business?

- How am I preparing the company for future challenges, technological changes, or market disruptions?

- Am I investing enough in innovation, talent development, and sustainability?

- Action: Set aside time to think about the long-term health of the company. Ensure that short-term pressures aren't causing you to lose sight of long-term objectives. Identify emerging trends or potential disruptions and plan.

6. Check Relationships with Key Stakeholders
Key Questions:

- How strong are my relationships with customers, investors, partners, and other stakeholders?

- Am I engaging with them to understand their needs and concerns?

- How do my decisions impact these relationships?

- Action: Reflect on how often you engage with stakeholders and how well you understand their evolving needs. The Importance of Open Communication

7. Track Personal Well-being and Resilience
Key Questions:

- How am I managing stress? Do I have a healthy work-life balance?

- Am I taking care of my mental and physical health?

- Do I have time for self-development and continuous learning?

- Action: assess your own well-being. Burnout can cloud judgment and reduce effectiveness as a leader. Focus on self-care, and make sure you are finding time to recharge. Commit to ongoing learning to stay sharp and adaptable.

8. Analyze How You Handle Failure and Success
Key Questions:

- How do I react when things go wrong? Do I take accountability, or do I blame others?

- How do I celebrate successes? Am I giving credit to the team or taking it for myself?

- Am I learning from failures and successes alike?

- Action: Reflect on your recent failures and successes. Be honest about how you handled them and what you learned from them. Failure offers some of the best opportunities for growth, so make sure you're turning missteps into learning experiences.

9. Reevaluate Innovation and Technology Strategy (CTO Focus)
Key Questions:

- Are we leveraging cutting-edge technology to stay competitive?

- How well are we aligning our tech roadmap with business goals?

- Is our development process agile enough to handle rapid changes in the market?

- Action: As CTO, reflect on the current state of the company's tech stack and innovation strategy. Are you investing in the right technologies? Are there inefficiencies in the development process? Be open to feedback from your tech teams and look for areas where improvements can be made.

10. Set Clear Goals for Continuous Improvement
Key Questions:

- What areas of my leadership need improvement? How can I set specific, measurable goals for personal and professional development?

- What feedback have I received that I haven't acted upon yet?

- How am I ensuring that the company, and my leadership, are always evolving?

- Action: Set personal and company-wide goals that reflect a commitment to growth. Consider hiring an executive coach or mentor to provide outside perspective and accountability. Be proactive about seeking new ways to improve and innovate.

Conclusion
Self-reflection helps you to stay grounded, aware, and adaptable in your leadership role as a CEO or CTO. By evaluating your decisions, leadership style, and impact, you can ensure that you continue to grow alongside your company. This is the importance of Self-Awareness

1.5.3 Anger
Anger and the Power of anger While it can be destructive if left unchecked, anger can also be a motivating force that spurs us to take action.

Anger over unfair job loss, anger at a partner during a relationship conflict, or anger about not receiving support.

1.5.3.1 Management Strategies: Channeling anger into positive action can be therapeutic. Techniques such as exercise, writing, or engaging in discussions can provide outlets for these feelings.

1.5.3.1 How to Improve Your Anger
Anger is a natural and sometimes necessary emotion that can signify that something in our lives needs attention. But, when anger becomes frequent or intense, it can have destructive effects on our relationships and health. Anger management strategies can offer to maintain control in heated situations.

1.5.3.2 Recognizing Triggers
Understanding what triggers your anger is the first step in managing it:

- Self-Observation: Pay attention to the situations, people, or feelings that provoke anger.

- Keep a Journal: Write down instances when you feel angry to identify patterns and triggers.

1.5.3.3 Relaxation Techniques
When you feel anger rising, use relaxation techniques to calm down:

- Deep Breathing Exercises: Focus on slow, deep breaths to help reduce physiological symptoms of anger.

1.5.3.4 Cognitive Restructuring
Change the way you think about situations that make you angry:

Challenge and Alter Negative Thoughts

1.5.3.5 How to Improve Your Communication Skills
Anger can cloud your ability to communicate, so improving your communication skills is key:

- Pause Before Speaking:
  Take a moment to collect your thoughts before responding in a heated situation.

- Use "I" Statements:
  Communicate your feelings and needs without blaming or criticizing others (e.g., frustrated when...").

1.5.3.6 Problem-Solving
Sometimes anger stems from real problems that one needs to address.

- Identify the Problem: define what is making you angry.

- Seek Solutions: Think about practical steps you can take to solve the problem rather than focusing on what made you angry.

1.5.3.7 Using Humor
Humor can help de-escalate anger:

- Lighten the Mood:
  Use humor to lighten the situation without belittling the seriousness of your feelings.

- Avoid Sarcasm: Be careful not to use humor that can be hurtful or sarcastic as it may worsen the situation.

1.5.3.8. Changing Your Environment
Sometimes the best way to reduce anger is to change your surroundings:

- Take a Break: Step away from situations or environments that elevate your stress.

- Create a Calm Space: Choose a place where you can go to calm down and feel relaxed.

1.5.3.9 Seeking Support
If anger is affecting your life, seeking help can be beneficial:

- Talk to a Friend: Sharing your feelings with someone can help you gain perspective and release pent-up emotions.

Consider seeking support from a counselor or therapist if your anger seems out of control or is affecting your relationships.

Conclusion
By adopting these strategies, you can begin to control your anger more, turning it from a destructive force into a constructive one.

1.5.4 Withdrawal
Withdrawal is a reaction where individuals pull away from others to avoid dealing with painful realities or emotions.

Many individuals Isolate themselves from social activities after a diagnosis such as Mental Health .

1.5.4.1 Management Strategies: Encouraging gentle but consistent social interaction can help.

How to Manage Withdrawal

- Isolation Is a Bad Idea Here are some strategies to manage and reduce unhealthy withdrawal behaviors:

- Recognizing the Signs of Unhealthy Withdrawal

The first step in managing withdrawal is to recognize its signs and understand when it becomes problematic:

- Social Isolation: Noticing a significant reduction in social interactions and avoiding gatherings.

- Loss of Interest: Losing interest in activities and hobbies that were once enjoyable.

- Increased Loneliness: Feeling lonelier and sadder the more time you spend alone.

1.54.2 Encouraging Gentle Social Interaction
Gradual reintroduction to social activities can help reduce feelings of isolation:

- Small Social Settings: Start with one-on-one meetups or small groups, which can be less overwhelming than large gatherings.

- Creating a Routine for Social Engagements

- Professional Support
  Professional help can be beneficial in understanding and overcoming the reasons behind withdrawal:

Therapists Can Help with Withdrawal.

1.5.4.3 Engage in Structured Activities
How to reduce the burden of social contact with structured activities

- Classes and Workshops:
  Enroll in a class or workshop that interests you. This provides both structure and an opportunity to meet new people with similar interests.

- Volunteering: Volunteering can offer a sense of purpose and community, and can be a less pressure-filled way to interact with others.

1.5.4.4 Developing Communication Skills
Improving how you communicate can make social interactions more rewarding and less stressful:

- Assertiveness Training: Learning to express your needs and boundaries-

- Improve Your Listening Skills

1.5.4.5 Mindfulness and Self-Compassion
Mindfulness and Self-Compassion Can Help With Withdrawal

Mindfulness Exercises for Beginners
Mindfulness is a practice that involves bringing attention to the present moment with an open and accepting attitude. For beginners, incorporating mindfulness exercises into daily life can help reduce stress, enhance

focus, and promote overall well-being. Here are some simple mindfulness exercises to get started:

1. Mindful Breathing

- How to Practice: Find a comfortable sitting or lying position. Close your eyes or soften your gaze. Take a deep breath in through your nose, allowing your abdomen to expand. Exhale slowly through your mouth. Continue this for a few minutes, focusing solely on your breath. If your mind wanders, gently bring your attention back to your breath.

- Duration: 5–10 minutes.

2. Body Scan

- How to Practice: Lie down comfortably on your back and close your eyes. Start by bringing your attention to your toes, noticing any sensations there. Gradually move your attention up your body (feet, legs, abdomen, chest, arms, neck, and head), observing any feelings of tension, relaxation, or discomfort without judgment.

- Duration: 10–15 minutes.

3. 5-4-3-2-1 Grounding Exercise

- How to Practice: This exercise helps bring you back to the present moment by engaging your senses.

- 5 things you can see: Look around and notice five things you hadn't paid attention to before.

- 4 things you can touch: Notice the texture of your clothing, the ground beneath your feet, or any objects around you.

- 3 things you can hear: Listen for sounds in your environment, such as birds chirping or distant traffic.

- 2 things you can smell: Inhale deeply and identify two scents in your surroundings (if you can't find any, think of your two favorite smells).

- 1 thing you can taste: Focus on the taste in your mouth or take a sip of water and notice its flavor.

- Duration: 5 minutes.

4. Mindful Eating

- How to Practice: Choose a small piece of food, like a raisin or a piece of chocolate. Before eating, observe its color, texture, and smell. Take a small bite and pay attention to the flavors and sensations in your mouth. Chew slowly and savor each bite, being aware of how it feels and tastes.

- Duration: 5–10 minutes.

5. Walking Meditation

- How to Practice: Find a quiet space where you can walk slowly, such as a garden or a quiet room. Walk at a comfortable pace, focusing on the sensation of your feet touching the ground. Notice the movement of your legs, the rhythm of your breath, and the environment around you. If your mind wanders, gently bring your focus back to your steps.

- Duration: 10–15 minutes.

6. Mindful Journaling

- How to Practice: Set aside a few minutes each day to write in a journal. Focus on your thoughts and feelings without judgment. You can write about your day, your emotions, or what you are grateful for. Allow your writing to flow freely, and don't worry about grammar or structure.

- Duration: 10 minutes.

7. Gratitude Practice

- How to Practice: At the end of each day, take a moment to reflect on three things you are grateful for. They can be big or small. Write them down or simply acknowledge them in your mind. This practice helps shift your focus to the positive aspects of your life.

- Duration: 5 minutes.

8. Guided Meditation

- How to Practice: Use a guided meditation app or online resource (such as Headspace, Calm, or Insight Timer) to find a beginner-friendly meditation. Follow the instructions to help you focus and relax.

- Duration: 10–15 minutes.

Tips for Success

- Start small: If you're new to mindfulness, begin with just a few minutes each day and gradually increase the duration as you become more comfortable.

- Be patient: Mindfulness is a skill that takes time to develop. It's normal for your mind to wander; gently bring your focus back without judgment.

- Create a routine: Incorporate mindfulness exercises into your daily routine, such as practicing in the morning, during lunch breaks, or before bed.

By integrating these mindfulness exercises into your daily life, you can cultivate a greater sense of awareness, reduce stress, and enhance your overall well-being. Enjoy the journey of mindfulness!

9. Lifestyle Adjustments
Making general lifestyle changes can also help manage withdrawal tendencies:

10. Exercises Can Improve Social Interactions

- Healthy Sleep Habits: Ensuring you get enough sleep can improve your mood and energy, making it easier to engage with others.

Conclusion
Withdrawal doesn't have to be a permanent state.

1.5.4.6 The Signs of Social Re-engagement
Social withdrawal can occur for various reasons, including mental health challenges, stress, trauma, or significant life changes. Recognizing the signs of social re-engagement after a period of withdrawal is essential for understanding one's recovery journey and fostering supportive relationships. Here are some common signs that indicate a person may be beginning to re-engage socially:

1. Increased Communication

- Description: The individual starts reaching out to friends and family through calls, texts, or social media. They may initiate conversations or respond more promptly to messages.

- Significance: This indicates a willingness to reconnect and share experiences with others.

2. Attending Social Events

- Description: The person begins to accept invitations to gatherings, parties, or other social events they previously avoided.

- Significance: Participating in social activities shows a desire to engage with others and enjoy shared experiences.

3. Expressing Interest in Others

- Description: The individual shows curiosity about others' lives, asking questions, and expressing concern or interest in their well-being.

- Significance: This reflects a shift from inward focus to a more outward perspective, indicating readiness to engage in relationships.

4. Initiating Plans

- Description: The person starts suggesting activities, such as going for coffee, attending events, or simply spending time together with friends or family.

- Significance: Taking the initiative to make plans signifies a commitment to rebuilding social connections.

5. Sharing Feelings and Thoughts

- Description: The individual becomes more open about their thoughts and feelings, discussing their experiences during the withdrawal period and expressing emotions.

- Significance: Sharing vulnerability fosters connection and trust, essential components of healthy relationships.

6. Engaging in Group Activities

- Description: The person may join clubs, classes, or support groups, participating in activities that involve interaction with others.

- Significance: Engaging in group activities demonstrates a readiness to connect with like-minded individuals and build a sense of community.

7. Positive Changes in Body Language

- Description: The individual exhibits more open and relaxed body language, such as maintaining eye contact, smiling, or engaging in active listening.

- Significance: Positive body language is often a reflection of emotional readiness to engage and connect with others.

8. Willingness to Seek Support

- Description: The person may reach out for help from friends, family, or professionals, showing a recognition of the importance of social support.

- Significance: Asking for support indicates a proactive approach to mental health and a desire to rebuild connections.

9. Increased Energy and Motivation

- Description: A noticeable increase in energy, motivation, or enthusiasm for activities can be a sign of re-engagement.

- Significance: Feeling more energized often correlates with a renewed interest in social interactions and activities.

10. Setting Boundaries

- Description: The individual begins to communicate their needs and boundaries more clearly, indicating a better understanding of their personal limits.

- Significance: Setting boundaries is a healthy way to engage socially while respecting one's own needs and well-being.

Conclusion
Recognizing these signs of social re-engagement can be encouraging for both the individual and their loved ones. It's essential to approach this process with patience and compassion, as re-engaging socially can take time and may involve setbacks. Supporting someone in their journey back to social interaction can foster a sense of belonging and connection, ultimately contributing to their overall well-being.

1.5.5 Sadness
Sadness is a complex emotional state characterized by feelings of unhappiness, sorrow, or despondency. It is a natural human emotion that everyone experiences at various points in life, often in response to specific events or situations. Here are some key aspects of sadness:

1. Nature of Sadness

- Emotional Response:
  Sadness can arise from a range of experiences, such as loss, disappointment, rejection, or loneliness. It may be triggered by external events, such as the death of a loved one, a breakup, or failure to achieve a goal.

- Temporary vs. Chronic:
  For many individuals, feelings of sadness are temporary and can be resolved over time. However, if sadness persists for an extended period or significantly impairs daily functioning, it may be indicative of a more serious condition, such as depression.

2. Physiological Effects

- Physical Symptoms:
  Sadness can manifest physically, leading to symptoms such as fatigue, changes in appetite, sleep disturbances, and decreased energy. It can also affect one's immune system, making individuals more susceptible to illness.

- Brain Activity:
  Research indicates that sadness can alter brain activity, particularly in areas associated with emotional regulation and processing, such as the amygdala(a part of the brain that blends with the media temporal cortex) and prefrontal (personality center) cortex. The amygdala is known for controlling fear and is important for survival

3. Cognitive Aspects

- Thought Patterns:
  Sadness often leads to a negative thought cycle, where individuals may ruminate on their feelings or dwell on past events. This can perpetuate feelings of hopelessness or helplessness.

- Perspective on Life: While sadness can provide a more somber view of life, it can also lead to deeper introspection and understanding of one's emotions and circumstances.

4. Social and Cultural Factors

- Expression of Sadness: Different cultures have varying norms regarding the expression of sadness. Some cultures encourage open expression of emotions, while others may promote stoicism.

- Support Systems:
  Social support plays a crucial role in how individuals cope with sadness. Friends, family, and community can provide comfort, understanding, and encouragement during difficult times.

5. Purpose of Sadness

- Adaptive Function: Sadness serves an adaptive function by prompting individuals to reflect on their circumstances, seek support, and make necessary changes in their lives. It can also foster empathy and connection with others who are experiencing similar emotions.

- Motivation for Change: Experiencing sadness can motivate individuals to address underlying issues, make amends in relationships, or pursue personal growth.

6. Coping with Sadness

- Healthy Coping Strategies: Individuals may cope with sadness through various means, such as talking to someone about their feelings, engaging in creative outlets, exercising, or practicing mindfulness and self-care.

- Seeking Professional Help: If sadness becomes overwhelming or persistent, it may be beneficial to seek help from a mental health professional, such as a therapist or counselor, who can provide support and guidance.

Conclusion
Sadness is a fundamental human emotion that reflects our responses to life's challenges and losses. While it can be uncomfortable and painful, it is an essential part of the emotional spectrum that contributes to our understanding of ourselves and our relationships. By acknowledging and processing sadness, individuals can find pathways to healing and personal growth.

1.5.5.1 Management Strategies:
Allowing oneself to grieve is important. Expressive activities like art, writing, or music can ease emotional expression and processing.

Sadness Management Strategies
Sadness is a natural emotional response to disappointment, loss, or other upsetting circumstances. While it's important to allow yourself to feel sad, lingering sadness can evolve into a deeper issue like depression if not managed. Here are some strategies to help you cope with and manage sadness in healthy ways:

1.5.5.2.Acknowledging and Accepting Your Feelings
The first step in managing sadness is to recognize and accept that it is okay to feel this way:

An Open Letter to Myself

- Understand It's Temporary: Remind yourself that sadness is a temporary state, and feelings will change over time.

1.5.5.3 Expressive Writing

- Writing can be a therapeutic way to manage feelings of sadness:- Journaling: Keep a daily journal to express your thoughts and feelings. Writing down what you are going through can bring clarity and relief.

- Letter Writing: Write letters to yourself or others (these don't have to be sent) to articulate feelings that might be hard to say out loud.

1.5.5.4 Physical Activity
Exercise can boost your mood and reduce symptoms of depression and sadness:

Boost Your Heart Rate With These Exercises

Practices like yoga combine physical movement with mindfulness can help reduce emotional intensity associated with sadness.

1.5.5.5 Social Support
Connecting with others can provide comfort and reduce feelings of isolation. Even if you don't feel like talking about your sadness, being around others can help.

1.5.5.6 Engaging in Enjoyable Activities
Participating in activities you enjoy can improve your mood and distract from sadness:

- Hobbies: Return to or discover new hobbies that bring you joy and satisfaction.

- Entertainment: Watch a favorite movie, read a good book, or listen to uplifting music.

1.5.5.7 Professional Help
If sadness persists and starts to interfere with your daily life, it might be time to seek professional help:

- Therapy: Talking to a therapist can provide insights into the underlying causes of your sadness and offer strategies to cope.

1.5.5.8 Mindfulness and Meditation
Practicing mindfulness and meditation can help you stay present and lessen the impact of negative thoughts:

1.5.5.9 Setting Routine and Goals
Creating a routine and setting small, achievable goals can provide structure and a sense of accomplishment:

- Daily Routines: Sleep, Meal, and Activity Schedule

- Small Goals: Set realistic goals each day or week, which can give you something to look forward to and focus on.

Conclusion
Sadness is a complex emotion that everyone experiences at some point. It's important to take action early and recognize when you need professional guidance to help you navigate through tougher times.

1.6 Mental Health and Resilience
Mental health and resilience are interconnected aspects of well-being. Mental health refers to the emotional, psychological, and social well-being that affects how, feel, and act. It includes managing stress, making decisions, forming relationships, and dealing with adversity.

Resilience, on the other hand is the ability to bounce back from difficult situations or crises. It does not mean avoiding stress or hardship but rather having the capacity to cope, adapt, and grow in the face of challenges.

1.6.1 Key factors that contribute to resilience include:

- Positive relationships and support networks
- A sense of purpose and meaning in life
- Adaptability and flexibility
- Self-regulation and emotional management skills
- A positive outlook and optimism

1.6.2 Mental Health and the Importance of Self Care

Mental health is crucial for well-being, influencing how we handle stress, relate to others, and make decisions in our daily lives. Self-care involves taking deliberate actions to care for our physical, emotional, and mental needs.

1.6.3 Why Self-Care is Important for Mental Health:

1. Self-Care Can Help Prevent Burnout are overwhelmed by stress and responsibilities. By taking breaks and nurturing ourselves, we ensure that we don't deplete our mental and emotional resources.

2. Enhances Emotional Resilience: Engaging in self-care activities helps build resilience.

3. The Importance of Self-Care Activities like meditation and connecting with loved ones can help boost happiness.

4. The Importance of Self-Care But, self-care replenishes our energy, making us more efficient and focused in daily tasks.

5. Supports Physical Health: Mental and physical health are intertwined. The Importance of Self-Care When we take care of our bodies, we improve our mental clarity, energy levels, and omit sense of well-being.

1.6.4 Types of Self-Care:
How to Practice Emotional Self-Care

- Social Self-Care: Building supportive relationships and staying connected with loved ones.

Incorporating self-care into daily life is not indulgent or selfish but essential for maintaining mental health. It's about finding balance and ensuring that you're meeting your own needs so you can be present and effective in other areas of life.

CHAPTER 2
Preparing for the Storms

As we navigate through life, encountering various storms is inevitable. Preparing for these challenges in advance can enhance our resilience and ability to cope.

2.1 How to Survive Adversity

2.1.1 Cultivating a Resilient Mindset
Here's how you can cultivate a resilient mindset:

- Optimism: Train yourself to look for the silver lining in difficult situations. This doesn't mean ignoring reality but rather focusing on what we can control and finding positive aspects where possible.

- Acceptance: Recognize that some situations are beyond your control. Accepting this fact can help you focus on your response rather than trying to change the unchangeable.

2.1.2 Building Resilience in a Crisis
Tools and Techniques for Building Resilience

Several practical tools can aid in enhancing your emotional and mental fortitude:

Here are some practical strategies:

2.2. Cultivate a Positive Mindset

- Practice Gratitude: reflect on what you're thankful for, which can shift your focus from what's wrong to what's going well.

- Focus on Strengths: Identify and use your personal strengths to overcome challenges. This boosts confidence and problem-solving skills.

2.3. Develop Strong Relationships

Surround yourself with friends, family, or mentors who offer support, encouragement, and perspective.

- Seek Help When Needed: Don't be afraid to ask for help or talk to a mental health professional when you're struggling.

2.4. Emotional Regulation Techniques

Mindfulness Meditation: Practicing mindfulness helps increase self-awareness

2.4.1 Journaling
Writing a journal is a simple yet powerful way to reflect on your thoughts, emotions, and experiences. It can improve mental clarity, help manage stress, and promote emotional well-being. Below are some steps to help you get started with journaling:

1. Choose Your Medium

- Traditional Paper Journal: Many people prefer writing by hand in a notebook or diary, as it can feel more personal and reflective.

BRIGHT SKIES AHEAD

- Digital Journal: If you prefer typing, use a computer, smartphone, or journaling app. This can be convenient and accessible.

- Hybrid: You can mix both methods depending on where you are or your mood on a particular day.

2. Set a Routine

- Pick a Time: Choose a specific time of day to journal. Many people journal in the morning to set their intentions for the day or in the evening to reflect on their experiences.

- Be Consistent: Regular journaling builds the habit. Even if you write for just 5-10 minutes a day, consistency is key.

- Start Small: You don't need to write for hours. Begin with a few sentences or paragraphs and build your practice.

3. Choose a Journaling Style
There are several ways to approach journaling depending on your goals and preferences:

How to Write This helps release pent-up thoughts or emotions.

- Gratitude Journaling: Focus on the things you're thankful for each day. Write down 3-5 things you're grateful for, which can shift your focus toward positivity.

- Reflective Journaling: Write about a particular event or experience and how it made you feel, what you learned, and how it affected you.

- Goal-Oriented Journaling: Document your goals, progress, and obstacles. Reflect on what steps you need to take to achieve your goals.

- Prompts-Based Journaling: Use journaling prompts or questions to guide your writing (e.g., "What are my biggest strengths?" or "How did today?").

4. Begin Writing

- Start with How You Feel: If you're unsure what to write, start by reflecting on your emotions. Ask yourself, "How am I feeling right now?" or "What has been on my mind?"

- Describe Your Day: Write about the events of your day, your interactions, and how they made you feel. Reflect on what went well and what could be improved.

- Ask Questions: Use questions to explore your thoughts, such as "What am I struggling with?" or "What am I proud of today?"

- Explore Solutions: If you're facing challenges, journal about possible solutions or ways to move forward. This can help you process and problem-solve.

5. Stay Honest and Authentic

- Write for Yourself: Your journal is for your eyes only (unless you choose to share it). Don't worry about how your writing sounds—focus on being open and honest with yourself.

- Express Your Emotions: Journaling is a safe space to release emotions, whether positive or negative. Writing down your feelings helps you process them in a healthy way.

6. Reflect and Revisit

- Review Entries Over Time:, revisit past entries to see how you've grown or to gain new insights into recurring themes in your life.

Journaling can help you better understand yourself and improve your emotional well-being.

7. Use Prompts (Optional)
If you ever feel stuck or unsure what to write about, try using prompts. Here are some ideas:

- What made me smile today?

- What am I grateful for right now?

- What are my biggest challenges at the moment?

- What do I want to do this week/month?

- How did in a particular situation, and why?

8. Be Kind to Yourself

- No Pressure: Don't worry about writing or producing long entries. It's okay if some days you only write a few sentences.

- Allow Breaks: If you miss a day (or a week), don't feel guilty. Journaling should be a helpful tool, not a rigid obligation.

- Celebrate Progress: Acknowledge and appreciate your efforts in journaling, even if it's small steps.

Benefits of Journaling:

- Reduces Stress: Journaling provides an outlet to express and release stress or negative emotions.

- Boosts Creativity: Writing can spark new ideas and creative thoughts.

- Enhances Self-Awareness: Through reflection, you become more aware of your habits, strengths, and areas for growth.

2.4.2 Anecdote-1.
Finding Light in the Shadows-the story Bammy using journaling to overcome the storms

When I was in my late twenties, I faced one of the hardest storms of my life: the sudden loss of my mother to a long battle with cancer. The news hit me like a thunderclap, leaving me in a haze of grief and disbelief. For months, I felt like I was walking through a dense fog, unable to see the way forward.

In the midst of this darkness, I discovered a small but powerful coping mechanism: journaling. I had never been particularly reflective or expressive through writing, but something compelled me to pick up a pen. Each night, I would sit in my room, pouring my heart onto the pages. I wrote about my pain, my memories of my mother, and the lessons she taught me. I wrote about the moments of joy we shared and the laughter that seemed so distant now.

As time passed, I began to notice a shift. What started as a release of sorrow transformed into a celebration of life. I began to write letters to my mother, sharing my daily experiences and the milestones I wished she could witness. This practice not only helped me process my grief but also kept her memory alive in my heart.

Additionally, I sought solace in nature. I took long walks in the park, allowing the fresh air and the beauty of the world around me to uplift my spirits. I found comfort in the changing seasons, realizing that as winter gives way to spring, my grief, too, would evolve into acceptance and hope.

Through these experiences, I learned that storms are a part of life, but they can lead to personal growth and resilience. I began to share my story with others, and in doing so, I connected with people who had faced their own storms. Each conversation became a reminder that we are not alone in our struggles, and that sharing our stories can be a source of strength.

Today, I still journal and make it a point to connect with nature whenever overwhelmed. My mother's spirit lives on in the stories I share, the lessons I apply, and the love I continue to give. Life's storms may be inevitable, but they can also lead us to brighter skies ahead if we allow ourselves to heal and grow.

2.5 Adaptability and Flexibility

- Embrace Change: Resilient people are flexible and can adapt to changing circumstances. Practice being open to new experiences and approaches.

- Set Realistic Goals: Break down big challenges into smaller, manageable steps. This makes it easier to stay focused and motivated.

- Learn from Mistakes: View failures as learning experiences, and focus on how you can grow from them.

2.6. Physical Self-Care

Physical self-care is a set of activities that improve your physical health. These include:

- Nutrition: Eating a balanced diet supports both physical and mental health, giving you the energy and focus to handle challenges.

- Hydration: Drinking enough water

- Exercise: Being active in a way that's fun and rewarding such as walking, playing a sport or yoga

- Sleep : Getting enough sleep which is usually between seven and eight hours

- Relaxation: Using relaxation Techniques like deep breathing or meditation

2.7 . Problem-Solving Skills

- Break Down Problems: Analyze challenges to understand the underlying issues, then brainstorm potential solutions.

- Stay Proactive: Don't wait for challenges to become overwhelming. Tackle problems early to prevent them from escalating.

- Manage What You Can Control: Focus on what you can influence, and accept that some things will be beyond your control.

2.8. Purpose and Meaning

- Clarify Your Values: Knowing what matters most to you can provide direction and motivation when facing adversity.

- Set Long-Term Goals: Having a sense of purpose helps to keep things in perspective and provides resilience during tough times.

- Volunteer or Help Others: Contributing to your community or helping those in need can give a sense of fulfillment and reinforce your sense of purpose.

2.9. Stress Management Techniques

- Progressive Muscle Relaxation (PMR): This technique involves tensing and then relaxing muscle groups to reduce physical tension.

- Visualization: Practice visualizing a calm, peaceful scene or imagining successful outcomes to promote a sense of control and relaxation.

- Time Management: Focus on tasks, set boundaries, and avoid overcommitting to reduce stress and build resilience.

2.10. Self-Compassion

- Be Kind to Yourself: Treat yourself with kindness and understanding during difficult times, rather than being critical.

- Practice Forgiveness: Learn to forgive yourself for mistakes or setbacks, which reduces unnecessary stress and guilt.

- Acknowledge Your Feelings: Allow yourself to experience and express emotions, rather than suppressing them.

2.11. Professional Support and Learning

- Counseling or Therapy: A mental health professional can help you develop coping strategies and build resilience.

- Join Support Groups: Being part of a community that faces similar challenges can offer new perspectives and emotional support.

- Lifelong Learning: learning new skills and gaining knowledge keeps you adaptable and able to face future challenges with confidence.

By applying these tools and techniques, individuals can strengthen their resilience over time, making them better equipped to face adversity and thrive in the long run.

2.12 Meditation to Improve Your Mental Health

Below is a step-by-step guide to help you get started with meditation and make it a regular practice:

1. Set Aside Time

    - Start Small: Begin with 5 to 10 minutes a day and increase the time as you become more comfortable with the practice.

    - Consistency Matters: Choose a time of day that works best for you and stick to it. Many people prefer to meditate in the morning to set a positive tone for the day, but any time that suits your schedule is fine.

2. Choose a Comfortable Space

    - Find a Quiet Spot: Select a quiet, calm space where you won't be disturbed. It could be a corner of your room, a balcony, or even a park.

    - Sit: Sit in a chair or on the floor with a cushion. You can cross your legs or keep them straight, as long as your posture is upright but relaxed. You don't have to sit in a traditional lotus position unless it's comfortable for you.

- Close Your Eyes: Closing your eyes can help cut distractions and allow you to focus inward.

3. Focus on Your Breath

- Deep Breathing: Start by taking a few deep breaths to relax. Inhale through your nose, allowing your belly to expand, then exhale through your mouth.

After a few deep breaths, let your breathing return to its natural rhythm. observe the sensation of your breath. Focus on the rise and fall of your chest or the feeling of air passing through your nostrils.

4. Be Present and Acknowledge Distractions

- Notice Your Thoughts: As you meditate, your mind will likely wander. This is completely normal.

- Label Thoughts: You can mentally label distractions to help release them (e.g., "thinking," "worrying," or "planning"), and then return to your breath.

5. Incorporate a Mantra or Visualization (Optional)

- Mantra Meditation: If you find it hard to focus on your breath, you can try repeating a word or phrase (mantra) in your mind. Common mantras include "peace," "calm," or "I am here."

- Visualization: You can also visualize a peaceful scene, such as a beach or a quiet forest, to help calm your mind and focus your thoughts.

6. Body Scan Meditation (Optional)

- Scan Your Body: During meditation, bring your awareness to different parts of your body, starting from your toes and moving up to your head. Notice any sensations, tension, or discomfort, and breathe into those areas to help release tension.

- Relax Tension: If you notice tightness in any area, focus on that part of the body and imagine it relaxing as you breathe.

7. Practice Mindfulness Throughout the Day

- Mindful Moments: Meditation can extend beyond formal practice. Try to incorporate mindfulness into your daily life by being present in everyday tasks.

How to Observe Without Judgment This builds emotional awareness and resilience.

8. End with Gratitude or Reflection

- Reflect on Your Practice: When you're ready to finish, open your eyes. Take a moment to notice how you feel and reflect on the practice without judgment.

- Gratitude: Express gratitude for taking time to care for your mental health. This positive reinforcement will encourage you to return to the practice.

Benefits of Meditation for Mental Health:

- Meditation helps lower cortisol (body's main stress hormone) levels and calms the mind, reducing anxiety and stress.

- Meditation Can Improve Your Productivity

- Meditation Can Improve Mental Health

- Meditation helps you become more aware of your thoughts and emotions..

Types of Meditation:

- Mindfulness Meditation: Focuses on being present and observing thoughts without judgment.

- Loving-Kindness Meditation (Mette): Focuses on developing compassion by sending thoughts of love and kindness to yourself and others.

- Transcendental Meditation: Involves repeating a mantra to calm the mind.

- Guided Meditation: Involves listening to a guide or recording that walks you through visualization or relaxation techniques.

Tips for Success:

- Be Patient: Don't expect immediate results. Meditation is a skill that improves with consistent practice.

- Don't Worry About "Clearing Your Mind": The goal isn't to stop thinking but to be aware of your thoughts without getting caught up in them.

- Stay Comfortable: If sitting becomes uncomfortable, adjust your position. The goal is to stay relaxed.

By practicing meditation, you can enhance your mental health, cultivate a sense of calm, and improve your ability to navigate life's challenges with resilience and mindfulness.

2.13 Setting Goals
Having clear, achievable goals provides direction and a sense of purpose.

The Importance of Setting Specific, Measurable, Achievable, Relevant, and Time-Bound (SMART) Goals

Setting SMART goals is a well-established practice that can enhance your likelihood of success. Let's break down what each component means in the context of purpose-driven goal setting:

Specific: Your goals should be clear and specific. Instead of setting a vague goal like "I want to help people," a more specific goal could be "I want to volunteer at a local food bank every weekend."

Measurable: A measurable goal allows you to track your progress. If your goal is to write a book, for instance, a measurable goal could be "I will write one chapter per week."

Achievable: While it's good to aim high, your goals should also be achievable. Consider your resources, constraints, and personal circumstances while setting your goals.

Relevant: Your should align your goals with your purpose. It could be 'I will reduce my carbon footprint by using public transportation's transportation.

Time-bound: Having a specific timeframe can provide motivation and create a sense of urgency. For example, "I will complete my online course in graphic design within six months."

SMART goals provide a clear roadmap towards your purpose, making the journey more focused and structured. They allow you to see progress, stay motivated, and celebrate milestones along the way. In the next section, we'll explore practical strategies to set and achieve these SMART goals.

2.13.1 Practical Tips for Goal Setting

Goal setting is a powerful process that requires thoughtfulness and commitment. Here are some practical tips to help you set effective goals:

- Write Your Goals Down: The act of writing down your goals makes them more tangible and reinforces your commitment to achieving them.

- Break Down Large Goals: Large or long-term goals can seem daunting. Break them down into smaller, manageable tasks or short-term goals. This makes the process less overwhelming and provides regular milestones to celebrate.

- Focus on Your Goals: If you have many goals, focus on them based on their relevance to your purpose and the impact they'll have on your life. Focus on one goal at a time to prevent feeling overwhelmed.

- Visualize Success: visualize yourself achieving your goals. This can boost motivation and make your goals feel more attainable.

- Review and Adjust: review your goals and progress. Don't hesitate to adjust your goals if your circumstances change or if you find them no longer aligned with your purpose.

- Seek Support: Share your goals with supportive friends, family, or mentors. They can provide encouragement, accountability, and advice.

- Practice Patience and Persistence: Achieving meaningful goals takes time. Be patient with your progress and persistent in your efforts. Remember, the journey towards your purpose is as important as the destination.

Setting goals is a dynamic process that keeps you focused on your path towards living your purpose. Through setting and achieving SMART goals, you'll move closer to fulfilling your life's purpose and creating a life that resonates with who you are.

2.14 Emotional Preparedness

Emotional preparedness involves recognizing and managing your feelings before they become overwhelming:

- Emotional Awareness: Learn to identify and label your emotions, which is the first step in managing them.

- Develop healthy ways to express your emotions, such as talking to a friend or engaging in creative activities.

2.15 Strengthening Social Networks
A strong support system is invaluable when facing life's storms:

- Strengthening Social Networks: Building a Robust Support System

Here are effective approaches to strengthen your social network.

A well-developed social network offers many benefits:

- Emotional Support: Social networks provide a listening ear and a source of comfort during challenging times.

- Practical Help: Friends and family can offer practical help, from running errands to providing expert advice.

2.15.1 Strategies for Strengthening Social Networks
Social Media Strategy:

1. Maintain Regular Communication

Staying in touch with people in your social network keeps relationships strong:

- Regular Check-Ins: Call, text, or meet with friends and family to maintain connections.

Video Calls and Social Media: How to Stay Connected

Celebrating Milestones

2. Build New Connections
Expanding your social network introduces fresh perspectives and opportunities for growth:

- Attend Social Events: Join gatherings and events where you can meet new people.

- Engage in Shared Interests: Find groups or clubs based on your hobbies to meet people with similar passions.

- Network: Attend industry events and conferences to build connections in your professional field.

2.15.2. Cultivate Deeper Relationships
Deepening relationships involves moving beyond surface-level interactions:

- Share Personal Stories: Open up about your experiences and emotions to foster deeper connections.

- Show Empathy: Practice active listening and show understanding of others' feelings and perspectives.

Create Shared Experiences with Friends and Family

2.15.3. Offer and Seek Support
You can build a robust social network is on reciprocity and mutual support:

- Offer Help: Extend a helping hand when someone in your network needs support.

- Seek Help: Don't hesitate to ask for help when needed—it's a sign of strength, not weakness.

Gratitude in Networking

2.15.4. Build a Diverse Network
A diverse social network provides a broader range of perspectives and resources:

- Include Different Backgrounds: Engage with people from various cultural, professional, and social backgrounds.

- Seek Mentorship: Build relationships with mentors who can offer guidance and wisdom.

Intergenerational Connections

2.15.5. Take part in Community Activities

- Volunteer: Join local volunteer groups or community service projects.

- Attend Local Events: Take part in community festivals, fairs, or charity events to meet new people and strengthen local ties.

Join Community Organizations

Conclusion
Strengthening social networks is a crucial step in building a resilient support system. You can create a robust social network that supports you through life's challenges. Strong connections will help you navigate difficult times and enjoy the journey along the way.

Build Connections: Invest time in nurturing relationships with family, friends, and colleagues. These connections can provide emotional support and practical help in times of need.

Take part in community groups or online forums where you can share experiences and gain support from others.

Connection provides emotional support, companionship, and a sense of belonging.

Meaningful connections play a critical role in our emotional well-being and resilience. They offer:

- Reduced Isolation: Building connections helps combat loneliness and creates a sense of community.

2.15.6 Strategies for Building Connections

Building connections takes effort and intentionality. Here are some effective strategies for cultivating meaningful relationships:

1. Be Open and Approachable

- Friendly Demeanor: Smile, make eye contact, and engage in light conversation to establish rapport.

- Active Listening: Show genuine interest in what others say by listening and asking follow-up questions.

2. Join Groups and Activities
Engaging in shared activities and interests

- Hobbies and Clubs: Join clubs or groups related to your interests, such as sports, book clubs, or gardening groups.

- Community Events: Attend local events and activities to meet people in your area.

- Volunteer Work: Volunteering connects you with others who share your values and commitment to service.

3. Nurture Existing Relationships
Maintaining and strengthening existing relationships is as important as building new ones:

- Regular Communication: Keep in touch with friends and family through calls, texts, or video chats.

- Quality Time: Spend quality time with loved ones, whether it's going out for a meal or having a simple conversation.

- Acts of Kindness: Show appreciation through small acts of kindness, like sending a thoughtful note or helping with a task.

4. Deepen Connections
Deepening connections involves moving beyond surface-level interactions to create meaningful relationships:

5. Develop a Connection Hub

- Empathy: Put yourself in others' shoes and acknowledge their feelings and perspectives.

- Shared Experiences: Engage in shared experiences that create lasting memories and strengthen bonds.

6. Build a Support Network
A support network consists of people who provide emotional and practical support when needed:

Identify Trusted Confidants

Diverse Support System: Build a network with a diverse range of skills and perspectives.

How to Build a Support Network

Conclusion
Building connections is an ongoing process that requires effort and genuine interest in others. By being open and approachable, you can create a strong network of meaningful relationships. These connections will not only enrich your life but also serve as a source of strength and support during life's storms.

2.3 Community Engagement: Service to Others
What is community engagement? Serving others can bring a sense of purpose, connect you with like-minded individuals, and create a positive

ripple effect. Here's how community engagement can be a powerful tool for overcoming life's storms and creating a more fulfilling life.

2.3.1 The Power of Giving Back

Service to others is a transformative experience that benefits both the giver and the recipient. When you engage in acts of kindness and service, you:

- Gain a Sense of Purpose: Helping others can give you a sense of purpose, especially during challenging times when you might feel lost or aimless.
  Giving back helps to Build Social Connections with the Community.

- Experience Gratitude: Serving others can increase your sense of gratitude.

2.3.2 Forms of Community Engagement

Community engagement can take many forms, depending on your interests and availability. Here are some ways to serve others:

- Charity Fundraiser: Fundraiser

Help others by sharing your skills and knowledge with us.

- Community Events: Take part in or organize community events like clean-up drives, charity runs, or local fundraisers.

2.3.3 Finding the Right Opportunities

Finding the right community engagement opportunities depends on your interests, skills, and availability. To discover the best ways to serve, consider:

- Your Skills: Use your unique skills to make a meaningful impact. For example, if you're a musician, consider performing at local events or teaching music to kids.

- Your Schedule: Choose opportunities that fit your schedule. Even small commitments, like volunteering a few hours a week, can make a big difference.

2.3.4. The Impact of Service on Personal Growth

Service to others can lead to personal growth and emotional healing. When you give back to your community, you can experience:

- Serving Others Helps You Through Hard Times

Enhanced Empathy: Interacting with People from Different Backgrounds

- Increased Resilience: Seeing the strength and courage of those you're helping can inspire you to overcome your own challenges.

2.3.5 Building a Culture of Service

To create a lasting impact, consider ways to encourage a culture of service in you

- Building a Culture of Service: Creating a Community of Compassion and Giving and empowered to give back to your communities.

2.3.6 Building a Community Service Culture

Here's how to create and sustain a culture of service that can make an Impact.

A culture of service has broad-reaching benefits for individuals, organizations, and communities:

- Creating a Stronger Community Bond

- Enhanced Personal Fulfillment: Serving others can bring a sense of purpose and satisfaction.

- Positive Social Impact: A culture of service leads to tangible improvements in the lives of those in need.

2.4 Strategies for Building a Culture of Service

Here are some effective strategies to cultivate a culture of service within your community or organization:

1. Lead by Example

Leaders play a critical role in fostering a service-oriented culture:

- Prove Commitment: Engage in volunteer activities and community service to set an example.

- Recognize Contributions: Acknowledge and celebrate those who contribute to the culture of service.

2.4.2. Create Opportunities for Service

Providing ample opportunities for community service encourages active participation:

- Organize Volunteer Events
  Developing a Community-Led Community Service and Service Group Involvement

2.4.3. Foster a Spirit of Collaboration

A collaborative approach to service encourages unity and teamwork:

- Work Together: Organize group activities that need collaboration and collective effort.

- Share Resources: Encourage resource sharing among community members to support service projects. This builds inclusivity in Service.

2.4.4. Emphasize Education and Awareness
Raising awareness about the importance of service can inspire greater involvement:

- Educational Workshops: Host workshops or seminars about the impact of community service.

- Awareness Campaigns: Launch campaigns to highlight the benefits of service and encourage participation.

- Storytelling: Share stories of positive change resulting from community service to inspire others.

2.4.5. Build Long-Term Partnerships
Establishing long-term partnerships with other organizations can strengthen the culture of service:Corporate Social Responsibility

Collaborating with Local Schools and Universities to Engage Students in Community Service

2.4.6. Recognize and Reward Service
Recognition of Service

Service Awards

Public Acknowledgment

Incentives for Participation

Conclusion
Building a Culture of Service can create a community where compassion and giving are valued and encouraged. Leading by example are valued and encouraged. This culture of service not only enriches the lives of those who give but also creates lasting positive change in the community.

CHAPTER 3:
Navigating Through the Storm

In this chapter, I explore the process of navigating through life's storms. When challenges strike, it's essential to have the right tools, strategies, and mindset to make it through to the other side.

3.1 Understanding the Storm
Every storm is unique, with its own set of challenges and complexities. To navigate through it, you must first understand the nature of the storm:

- The Source: Determine the underlying causes of the challenge. Consider how this storm is affecting your life, including emotional, physical, and financial well-being.

- Recognize and accept the range of emotions you may be experiencing, from fear to sadness.

3.2 Taking Control of What You Can
While you may not be able to control the storm itself, you can control your response to it. Here are some practical steps to regain control:

- Establish a Routine: Having a daily routine can provide structure and stability during chaotic times.

- Set Small Goals: Break down big challenges into manageable steps, allowing you to make steady progress.

- Focus on What You Can Change: Direct your energy towards areas where you can make a difference, rather than dwelling on what you can't control.

3.2.1 Seeking Support and Connection
Navigating through a storm is much easier when you have a strong support network:

- Reach Out for Help: Don't hesitate to ask for support from friends, family, or professionals. It shows strength, not weakness.

Join a Support Group

Stay Connected: How to Stay Connected to Your Community

3.2.2 Developing Coping Mechanisms
Developing healthy coping mechanisms is key to enduring the storm and emerging stronger:

- Engage in Physical Activity: Regular exercise can boost your mood and energy levels, helping you manage stress.

3.2.3 Key Lessons for Navigating Through the Storm
Navigating through life's storms can be challenging, but there are key lessons that can help you weather difficult times with resilience and grace. Here are some important lessons to consider:

1. Embrace Change

- Acceptance: Recognize that change is a part of life. Accepting it can help you adapt more easily to new circumstances.

- Flexibility: Be willing to adjust your plans and expectations. Adaptability is crucial in turbulent times.

2. Cultivate Resilience

- Inner Strength: Understand your capacity to recover from setbacks. Focus on your strengths and past successes.

- Problem-Solving Skills: Develop a proactive mindset. Instead of dwelling on problems, think about potential solutions.

3. Stay Present

- Mindfulness: Practice being in the moment. This can help reduce anxiety about the future and regrets about the past.

- Breathe: Use deep breathing techniques to calm your mind and body, especially during stressful situations.

4. Seek Support

- Reach Out: Don't hesitate to lean on friends, family, or professionals. Sharing your struggles can lighten the burden.

- Community: Engage with a community or support group. Connecting with others who understand can provide comfort and guidance.

5. Maintain a Positive Outlook

- Focus on the Silver Lining: Look for lessons or opportunities for growth in every challenge. Positivity can be a powerful motivator.

- Gratitude: Practice gratitude to shift your perspective. Acknowledging what you have can foster hope and resilience.

6. Prioritize Self-Care

- Physical Health:Maintain a healthy lifestyle through exercise, proper nutrition, and adequate sleep. Physical well-being supports emotional strength.

- Mental Health:Engage in activities that nourish your mind, such as hobbies, meditation, or reading.

7. Set Realistic Goals

- Break It Down:When facing overwhelming challenges, break your goals into smaller, manageable tasks. This can make the journey feel less daunting.

- CelebrateProgress:Acknowledge and celebrate your achievements, no matter how small. This can boost your motivation.

8. Learn from Experience

- Reflect:Take time to reflect on past challenges and what you learned from them. This can provide valuable insights for future storms.

- Growth Mindset:Adopt a mindset that views challenges as opportunities for growth rather than as insurmountable obstacles.

9. Practice Patience

- Give Yourself Time:Healing and recovery take time. Be patient with yourself as you navigate through difficulties.

- Trust the Process:Understand that storms eventually pass, and brighter days will come. Trust that you are moving in the right direction.

10. Find Meaning

- Purpose:Reflect on your values and what gives your life meaning. Finding purpose can provide motivation during tough times.

- Legacy:Consider how you want to be remembered or what impact you want to leave on others. This can guide your actions during storms.

Conclusion
Navigating through life's storms is a journey that requires patience, resilience, and support. You can find your way through the darkness and emerge stronger on the other side. By understanding the nature of the storm, you can take control of what you can. This chapter provides you with the tools and inspiration to face your challenges head-on, knowing that brighter skies are ahead.

3.2.4 Engage Family and Friends in Community Service
Engaging family and friends in community service can be a rewarding experience that strengthens bonds while making a positive impact in your community. Here are some ideas and strategies to effectively involve your loved ones in community service activities:

1. Identify Common Interests

- Discuss Passions:Have a conversation with family and friends about causes they care about (e.g., animal welfare, environmental conservation, education, homelessness).

- ChooseTogether:Collaboratively select a cause or project that resonates with everyone involved.

2. Plan a Group Activity

- Volunteer as a Team:Organize a one-time or ongoing volunteer opportunity where everyone can participate together, such as serving at a local food bank, participating in a park cleanup, or helping at a community garden.

- Host a Fundraiser:Plan a group fundraising event, like a bake sale, car wash, or charity run, to raise money for a cause you all support.

3. Make it Fun and Engaging

- Incorporate Games:Turn volunteering into a fun activity by incorporating games or friendly competitions. For example, see who can collect the most litter during a cleanup.

- Create a Family Challenge:Set a challenge for your family or friends to complete a certain number of volunteer hours over a month or year.

4. Educate and Raise Awareness

- Host Informational Sessions:Organize gatherings where you can learn more about specific issues affecting your community, inviting guest speakers or watching documentaries.

- Share Stories:Encourage family members to share their experiences and insights related to community service, fostering a deeper understanding of the impacts of their contributions.

5. Make it Regular

- Establish a Routine:Create a regular schedule for community service, such as monthly volunteer days, to encourage ongoing commitment and participation.

- Create a Family Service Tradition: Consider starting a tradition, like volunteering together during holidays or special occasions, to make it a meaningful part of your family culture.

6. Leverage Social Media

- Share Experiences:Use social media to document and share your community service experiences, inspiring others to join or participate.

- Create a Group Page:Set up a private group on social media where you can share opportunities, plan events, and celebrate each other's contributions.

7. Involve Children

- Family Friendly Activities:Choose age-appropriate volunteer opportunities that children can participate in, like assembling care packages or participating in youth-led environmental projects.

- Teach Values:Use community service as a way to teach children about empathy, kindness, and the importance of giving back.

8. Connect with Local Organizations

- Research Opportunities:Look for local nonprofits or community organizations that offer group volunteering options. Many organizations welcome families and groups.

- Offer Your Skills:Identify skills within your group that could benefit a nonprofit, such as marketing, event planning, or tutoring.

9. Recognize Contributions

- Celebrate Achievements: Take time to acknowledge and celebrate the efforts of everyone involved, whether through a small gathering or a group outing.

- Share Impact Stories: Regularly communicate the impact of your collective efforts, helping everyone see the difference they are making in the community.

10. Lead by Example

- Demonstrate Commitment: Show your dedication to community service through your actions. Your enthusiasm and commitment can inspire others to get involved.

- Invite Participation: Whenever you engage in community service, invite family and friends to join you, making it clear that their participation is valued.

Conclusion
Engaging family and friends in community service not only strengthens relationships but also fosters a sense of shared purpose and commitment to making a difference. By creating enjoyable, meaningful experiences, you can inspire those around you to actively participate in serving the community. Volunteering, mentoring, or organizing community events can transform your life and the lives of those around you.

3.2.5 Psychological First Aid
Mental first aid is crucial for mental health emergencies

- Self-Care Techniques: Learn techniques like deep breathing, relaxation, and self-soothing to help manage stress on the spot.

When to See a Mental Health Professional are sometimes recommended.

3.2.6 Regular Practice and Preparation
Like any skill, resilience strengthens with practice:

- Regular Review and Practice: review the tools and strategies you've learned and practice them even in times of calm. This preparation makes it easier to apply them during crises.

Conclusion
Preparing for life's storms isn't about preventing them, but about equipping yourself with tools and skills to manage and overcome them. By fostering resilience, nurturing your support networks, you can face challenges with confidence.

3.3 Mindset Shifts: Concepts for Embracing Change and Building Resilience
A mindset shift involves changing the way you think about and react to situations.

Mindset Shift and your abilities and intelligence can be developed through dedication and hard work. Embracing a growth mindset involves:

Using Challenges as Opportunities

- Embracing Feedback: Use feedback as a tool for learning, rather than a personal critique.

- Perseverance in the Face of Setbacks: Understand that mastery takes time and effort, and setbacks are part of the learning process.

3.3.2. Gratitude Orientation

Focusing on gratitude involves shifting your attention from what's missing or wrong to what's present and right. This can enhance your life satisfaction by:

- Keeping a Gratitude Journal can shift your focus from negative to positive aspects of your life.

-How to Express Appreciation to Others

3.3.3. Enough Mindset

Plenty Mindset vs Scarcity Mindset This mindset encourages:

- Generosity: Sharing your resources, believing that there is enough to go around.

- Openness to Possibilities: Seeing life's possibilities, rather than its limitations.

3.3.4. Acceptance and Commitment

Accepting Things as They Are :Key practices include:

- Mindful Awareness: Being aware of the present moment without judgment.

- Value-driven Actions: Identifying what matters to you and taking actions that reflect these values.

3.3.5. Compassionate Mindset

Developing compassion for yourself and others can transform the way you experience life's challenges. It involves:

- Self-Compassion: How to Be Kind to Yourself

- How to Improve Your Relationships with Others

3.3.6. Solution-Focused Thinking
Instead of dwelling on problems, solution-focused thinking emphasizes finding effective solutions. This includes:

- Identifying What Works: Focus on strategies and actions that have before led to successful outcomes.

- Setting Clear Goals: Define what success looks like and work towards achieving these goals.

3.3. 7. Adaptive Thinking
What is Adaptive Thinking? It includes:

Cognitive Flexibility

- Problem Re-framing: Changing the way a problem is viewed to find new solutions or reduce its emotional impact.

Conclusion
Mindset shifts are powerful tools for personal growth and resilience. You can enhance your ability to cope with adversity, embrace change and navigate the complexities of life. Each of these mindset shifts offers a pathway to not only survive but thrive during the storms of life.

3.4 Tools and Strategies for Navigating Life's Challenges
To navigate life's challenges, you need a diverse set of tools and strategies. These can help you cope with stress, build resilience, and stay on course even when the going gets tough. Here are some of the most effective tools and strategies for overcoming life's storms.

3.4.1. Mindfulness and Meditation

Mindfulness involves being present and aware of your thoughts and feelings without judgment. Meditation, a subset of mindfulness, can help you calm your mind and reduce stress. Techniques include:

- Breathing Exercises: Focus on deep, slow breaths to calm your body and mind.

- Body Scan Meditation: Mentally scan your body from head to toe, noticing areas of tension and relaxing them.

- Guided Visualization: Use guided imagery to create a peaceful mental space where you can relax and rejuvenate.

3.4.2. Cognitive Behavioral Techniques

Cognitive Behavioral Therapy (CBT) focuses on identifying and changing negative thought patterns. Some effective CBT strategies include:

- Cognitive Restructuring: Challenge irrational beliefs and replace them with more balanced thoughts.

Behavioral Activation

- Exposure Therapy: expose yourself to feared situations to reduce avoidance behaviors.

3.4.3. Goal Setting and Time Management

Setting clear, achievable goals and managing your time can help you stay on track during challenging times:

- SMART Goals: Make goals Specific, Measurable, Achievable, Relevant, and Time-bound.

- Task Prioritization: Focus on tasks to focus on what's most important.

3.4.4. Social Support Systems
Connecting with others provides emotional support and practical help during difficult times:

- Building a Support Network

- Mentoring and Coaching: Seek guidance from mentors or coaches who can offer advice and support.

3.4.5. Physical Health and Wellness
Maintaining physical health is key to managing stress and building resilience:

- Regular Exercise: Engage in regular physical activity to boost mood and energy levels.

- Balanced Diet: Eat a balanced diet rich in fruits, vegetables, and whole grains to support omit health.

- Adequate Sleep: Ensure you get enough sleep to maintain energy and emotional stability.

3.4.6. Creative Outlets
Creative activities can provide an outlet for stress and a way to express emotions:

- Artistic Expression: Engage in drawing, painting, or other artistic pursuits to channel emotions.

- Music and Dance: Listen to music or dance to uplift your spirits and reduce stress.

- Creative Writing: Write stories, poetry, or journal entries to express thoughts and feelings.

3.4.7. Problem-Solving and Decision-Making Skills
Developing Effective Problem Solving and Decision Making Skills

Using SWOT Analysis to Solve Problems

- Decisiveness: Learn to make decisions with confidence, even when faced with uncertainty.

- Seeking Feedback: Don't hesitate to ask for input from others to gain different perspectives.

Conclusion
By using these tools and strategies, you can better navigate life's storms and maintain a positive outlook. While it's impossible to avoid all challenges, these approaches can help you cope with them more and recover more. Having a diverse toolkit enables you to tackle whatever life throws your way.

3.5 Learning from Real-Life Stories
Real-Life Lessons: Diverse Stories of Resilience and Triumph

These real life stories exemplify how to :

- Overcome a Major Obstacle

- Finding Hope in Difficult Times

- Turning Pain into Purpose

In this section, we'll share stories of real people who faced significant storms in their lives and found ways to overcome them. The Power of Resilience

3.5.1 Story 1: Rebuilding After a Natural Disaster
Jummy's Journey

Jummy lived in a coastal town which experience a heavy flood that destroyed her home and she lost most of her possessions. Despite this, Jummy's spirit remained unbroken. Here's how she rebuilt her life:

- Seeking Support: Jummy reached out to her community for help. Neighbors, friends, and local organizations came together to provide shelter, food, and clothing.

- Rebuilding Step-by-Step: Instead of focusing on the size of her loss, Jummy broke down the rebuilding process into manageable steps. She started by finding a temporary place to live and worked on rebuilding her home.

- Giving Back: Even as she was rebuilding her life, Jummy volunteered to help others in her community who were also affected by the flood. This act of service gave her a sense of purpose and strengthened her bonds with others.

3.5.2 Story 2: Overcoming a Major Health Challenge
John's Triumph

John, a young athlete, was diagnosed with a rare form of cancer that threatened to end his sports career. The news was devastating, but John found a way to stay positive and fight back:

- Maintaining a Positive Mindset: John refused to let his diagnosis define him. He focused on the things he could control, such as his attitude and his dedication to treatment.

- Building a Support Network: John relied on his family, friends, and medical team for support. They encouraged him through the toughest times and celebrated every small victory.

John discovers a love for painting and photography. These creative outlets helped him cope with the emotional toll of his illness.

3.5.3 Story 3: Turning Loss into Purpose
Adana's Transformation

Adana's life changed forever when she lost her spouse in a tragic accident. Grief overwhelmed her, and she felt lost without her partner. But Adana found a way to turn her pain into purpose:

Adana allows herself to grieve. That helped her understand that grief is a process and that healing takes time. Adana started a foundation that supported causes her partner cared about. This gave her a new sense of purpose and allowed her to create something positive from her loss.

- Supporting Others: Adana used her experience to help others who were grieving. She volunteered with local bereavement groups and shared her story to inspire others to find hope after loss.

3.5.4 Story 4: Finding New Beginnings After Financial Ruin
David's Resilience

David's business failed, leaving him with significant debt and uncertainty about the future. He felt defeated but found a way to rebuild his life:

Taking Responsibility: David's Financial Situation

- Learning New Skills: To reinvent himself, David enrolled in courses to learn new skills. This helped him transition to a new career and regain his confidence.

- Embracing Humility: Instead of dwelling on his failure, David used it as a learning opportunity. He shared his story with others to help them avoid similar mistakes and became a mentor for aspiring entrepreneurs.

3.5.5. Finding hope in people and God - The story of Nikky
Growing up without the love of a father and being the victim of transferred aggression due to love gone sour is every girl's worst dream. Not to talk of the label of a witch 'endowed' on me because of my father's relentless pursuit of a life free from his 'witch wife' in the hands of seers and their likes.

This exposed me to all forms of abuse because the dysfunctional home setting had me live with people during my formative years. Not only was I a withdrawn child, I had spiralled into huge depth of depression without anyone knowing and even years before the clinical diagnosis.

How have I coped? My Faith in God, being around people who believe in me, and learning to receive love from people and the Almighty God.

Conclusion
These stories illustrate that no matter the storm you face, there's a way through it. As you navigate through your own challenges, remember that you are not alone. There are stories of strength and courage all around you, offering hope and inspiration.

3.6 Key Lessons: Strategies for Navigating Through Life's Storms
Navigating through life's storms requires resilience, determination, and effective strategies. From the diverse stories shared, we can extract key lessons and strategies that can guide you through challenging times. Let's break them down into actionable insights.

3.6.1. Seek Support and Connection

Support from others is crucial when navigating through storms.

Strategies to seek support include:

- Reach Out to Trusted Friends and Family: Don't hesitate to ask for help or share your struggles with those you trust.

Join Support Groups to build

Strong Relationships

3.6.2. Focus on What You Can Control

When storms arise, focus on areas where you can make a difference. Strategies for this mindset include:

- Establish a Routine: Structure your day to create stability during uncertain times.

- Concentrate on Positive Habits: Engage in activities that promote physical and mental well-being.

3.6. 3. Develop Healthy Coping Mechanisms

Healthy coping mechanisms help you stay resilient during difficult times. Strategies for coping include:

- Practice Mindfulness and Meditation: These techniques can reduce stress and increase focus.

- Engage in Physical Activity: Exercise can boost your mood and energy levels.

- Find Creative Outlets: Pursue hobbies or creative activities that help you express your emotions.

3.6.4. Learn from Challenges

Every storm offers an opportunity for growth and learning. Strategies for extracting lessons from challenges include:

- Reflect on Your Experiences: Take time to understand what you c learn from your struggles.

- Embrace Change: See change as a chance to grow and evolve, rather than something to fear.

- Seek Feedback: Ask for feedback from trusted sources to identify areas for personal improvement.

3.6.5. Build a Resilient Mindset

A resilient mindset can help you weather any storm. Strategies for building resilience include:

- Stay Positive: Focus on the positives in your life, even during difficult times.

- Be Adaptable: Remain open to new approaches and solutions to navigate challenges.

- Maintain Hope: Keep sight of the fact that storms pass, and brighter days lie ahead.

3.5.6. Engage in Service and Giving Back

Engaging in acts of service can provide a sense of purpose and connection. Strategies for building a culture of service include:

- Volunteer: Take part in community service activities to give back and strengthen connections.

- Support Others in Need: Offer help to those facing challenges, knowing that kindness creates a positive ripple effect.

- Promote a Culture of Service: Encourage others to engage in service, creating a communityfocused on compassion and giving.

Conclusion
These key lessons and strategies can guide you through life's storms, helping you stay resilient, focused, and hopeful. You can navigate through the toughest of times and emerge stronger on the other side. How to cope with mental health challenges Keep these strategies in mind as you continue your journey toward brighter skies ahead.

3.7 Personal Anecdotes : Finding Support During Challenging Times
Finding support during challenging times can make all the difference in how we cope with adversity. Personal anecdotes serve as powerful reminders of the importance of reaching out to others. Here are some stories that show the transformative power of support.

3.6.1 Story 1: A Friend's Compassion in a Time of Loss
Kelly's Story

When Kelly lost his job, he was overwhelmed by a sense of failure and uncertainty about the future. The financial strain added to his stress, and he found it difficult to stay positive. His friend, Razaq, noticed his struggles and reached out with a simple gesture: an invitation to coffee. What's Next for Kelly?

Razaq's support was invaluable. He connected Kelly with a former colleague who was hiring, helping him find a new job within weeks. This act of compassion showed Kelly that he wasn't alone and that support can come from unexpected places.

3.6.2 Story 2: The Strength of Family During a Health Crisis
Linda's Story

Linda's life changed when she was diagnosed with a serious illness. The treatments were intense, and she faced long stays in the hospital. Her family became her anchor during this challenging time. Her husband took over many of the household responsibilities, and her children visited her.

One of the most touching moments was when Linda's family organized a small party in her hospital room to celebrate her birthday. This simple act reminded her that, despite the illness, she had a network of people who loved and supported her. It was their encouragement and presence that helped her stay strong throughout her recovery.

3.6.3 Story 3: A Community's Support After a Natural Disaster
Betty's Story

Betty's neighborhood was damaged by a hurricane. The storm destroyed homes and left many families without basic necessities. The community rallied together to support each other. Betty, who had lost her home, was overwhelmed by the outpouring of help. Neighbors shared food, water, and shelter with those in need, creating a sense of solidarity and compassion.

What stood out most to Betty was the sense of unity among her neighbors. They organized 3.community clean-up events and worked together to rebuild their homes. This collective effort not only helped Betty and others recover but also created a stronger sense of community.

3.6.4 Story 4: Finding Support in Unexpected Places
Adiva's Story

Adiva faced a difficult divorce that left her feeling isolated and unsure about her future. She found support in an unexpected place: a local yoga class. The instructor, who had also gone through a divorce, shared her own story of recovery and resilience. Adiva found comfort in the camaraderie and encouragement of the yoga community.

A Divorce Survivor built Friendships with Other People. This newfound community helped her regain her confidence.

Conclusion
These personal anecdotes highlight the importance of finding support during challenging times. A community that rallies together can be a beacon of hope in the midst of a storm. These stories show that even in the darkest of times, there's light to be found in the connections we make and the support we give and receive.

CHAPTER 4:
Embracing Change— Exploring the Concept of Change and Growth During Difficult Times

Change is an inevitable part of life, and embracing it can be challenging, especially during difficult times. This chapter explores the concept of change, highlighting how it can be a catalyst for personal growth and transformation. Change can be unsettling, how to navigate through transitions, and why embracing change can lead to a richer, more fulfilling life.

4.1 The Nature
Change is the process of becoming different, and it often requires us to adapt to new circumstances ..We must understand The nature of change because it helps us appreciate its potential for growth and transformation.

- External Triggers: Events like job loss, moving to a new location, or a major life event can bring about external changes that need adaptation.

Personal growth, evolving interests, or shifts in values can lead to internal changes.

4.1.1 Why Change Can Be Challenging

Change can evoke a range of emotions and reactions. Here are some common reasons why change can be difficult:

- Fear of the Unknown: Change often involves uncertainty, which can lead to fear and anxiety about what lies ahead.

The Disruption of Comfort Zones

- Loss and Grief: Change sometimes involves loss, whether it's a person, a job, or a way of life, which can trigger grief and sadness.

4.1.2 Embracing Change as a Path to Growth

Despite the challenges, embracing change can lead to personal growth and new opportunities. Here's why embracing change can be transformative:

- New Hires & Career Opportunities

- Adaptability and resilience

- Embracing Change Can Lead to a Deeper Understanding of Oneself and One's Values

4.2 Strategies for Embracing Change

To embrace change and use it as a catalyst for growth, consider these strategies:

1. Acknowledge and Accept Change
Acceptance is the first step in embracing change:

- Recognize the Reality: Acknowledge that change is happening and that it's a natural part of life.

- Accept Your Emotions: Allow yourself to feel the emotions that come with change, whether it's fear, sadness, or uncertainty.

- Let Go of Resistance: Resistace to change can create extra stress. Instead, focus on adapting to the new reality.

2. Reframe Change as an Opportunity
Shifting your perspective on change can help you see it as a positive force:

- Identify the Potential: Look for the opportunities that change brings, such as new experiences or personal growth.

- Focus on What You Gain: Instead of dwelling on what you've lost, focus on the new skills, relationships, or insights that change can offer.

- Embrace the Challenge: View change as a challenge that can help you grow stronger and more adaptable.

3. Build a Support System
A strong support system can make embracing change easier:

- Identify and Keep Supportive People

- Talk about your journey through change

3.1 What to Do When You're Feeling Overwhelmed.
Feeling overwhelmed is a common experience, and it's important to have strategies to help manage those feelings. Here are several actionable steps you can take when you find yourself in this situation:

1. Pause and Breathe

- Deep Breathing:Take a few moments to practice deep breathing. Inhale slowly through your nose, hold for a few seconds, and exhale through your mouth. Repeat several times to calm your mind and body.

- Mindfulness:Spend a few minutes focusing on the present moment. Pay attention to your surroundings, sensations, or sounds. This can help ground you.

2. Identify Triggers

- Reflect:Take a moment to identify what is causing your feelings of overwhelm. Is it work, personal issues, or too many commitments?

- Write It Down:Journaling your thoughts can help clarify what you're feeling and why. This can also provide a sense of relief.

3. Break Tasks into Smaller Steps

- Prioritize: List out your tasks and prioritize them based on urgency and importance. Focus on what needs immediate attention.

- Chunking:Break larger tasks into smaller, manageable steps. This can make them feel less daunting and more achievable.

4. Set Boundaries

- Learn to Say No:If you're taking on too much, consider saying no to additional commitments. Protect your time and energy.

- Limit Distractions: Identify distractions that may be contributing to your overwhelm and minimize them. This could include turning off notifications or designating specific times for tasks.

5. Practice Self-Care

- Take Breaks:Step away from your tasks for a short while. A quick walk, stretching, or simply sitting in silence can refresh your mind.

- Engage in Activities You Enjoy: Spend time doing something you love, whether it's reading, exercising, or spending time with friends or family.

6. Reach Out for Support

- Talk to Someone:Share your feelings with a friend, family member, or colleague. Sometimes, just expressing what you're going through can provide relief.

- Seek Professional Help:If feelings of overwhelm persist, consider speaking with a therapist or counselor who can provide guidance and coping strategies.

7. Limit Information Overload

- Take Breaks from Technology: Step away from screens and social media for a while. Constant notifications and information can contribute to feelings of overwhelm.

- Curate Your Inputs: Be selective about what you consume in terms of news, social media, and other content. Limit exposure to negative or stressful information.

8. Practice Gratitude

- Focus on Positives:Take a moment to reflect on what you're grateful for. This can shift your mindset and help you see beyond the overwhelm.

- Gratitude Journal: Consider keeping a gratitude journal where you jot down a few things you appreciate each day.

9. Engage in Physical Activity

- Exercise: Physical activity can be a great way to release pent-up energy and reduce stress. Even a short walk can make a difference.

- Stretching or Yoga: Incorporating stretching or yoga into your routine can help relieve tension and promote relaxation.

10. Create a Relaxation Routine

- Establish a Wind-Down Ritual: Develop a routine that helps you relax at the end of the day, such as reading, meditating, or taking a warm bath.

- Practice Relaxation Techniques: Explore techniques such as progressive muscle relaxation, guided imagery, or meditation apps.

Conclusion
Feeling overwhelmed is a natural response to stress, but it's essential to take proactive steps to manage those feelings. By incorporating some of these strategies into your routine, you can regain a sense of control and calm. Remember that it's okay to ask for help and take time for yourself.

4. Focus on Personal Growth
Embracing change can be a journey of personal growth and self-discovery:

- Set New Goals: Use change as an opportunity to set new personal or professional goals that align with your evolving values.

- Develop New Skills: Learn new skills or pursue new hobbies that can help you adapt to changing circumstances.

- Reflect on Your Journey: Take time to reflect on how change has influenced your personal growth and what you've learned from the experience.

Conclusion
Embracing change can be a powerful path to personal growth and transformation. Building a support system can help you navigate through transitions. While it can be challenging, accepting change, reframing it as an opportunity can be an opportunity. Remember that change is a constant in life, and by embracing it, you open yourself to new possibilities, insights, and experiences. This chapter serves as a guide to help you embrace change and use it as a stepping stone to a brighter and more fulfilling future.

4.3 Strategies for Embracing Change and Finding Opportunities for Growth

How to Embrace Change as a Career Changer can help you navigate the uncertainty and harness change to your advantage. Here's a comprehensive guide to embracing change and discovering new opportunities for growth.

4.3.1. Cultivate a Growth Mindset
A growth mindset is key to embracing change and seeking opportunities for development. Here's how to cultivate it:

- Embrace Learning: See every change as an opportunity to learn and grow. Approach challenges with curiosity and a willingness to adapt.

- Make the Most of Your Mistakes
  Making the most of your mistakes is about shifting your perspective from viewing errors as failures to seeing them as valuable learning opportunities. Here's a short perspective on how to do that:

- Embrace a Growth Mindset
  Mistakes are a natural part of the learning process. Embracing a growth mindset means understanding that abilities and intelligence can be developed through effort and experience.

- Reflect and Analyze
  Instead of dwelling on what went wrong, take time to reflect on the situation. Analyze what led to the mistake and identify lessons learned. This reflection can provide insights that help you avoid similar errors in the future.

- Take Responsibility
  Owning your mistakes fosters accountability. Acknowledge your role in the situation and consider how you can improve. This empowers you to make changes and take proactive steps moving forward.

- Adjust Your Approach
  Use your mistakes to inform your future decisions. Adjust your strategies based on what you learned, and be open to trying new approaches that might yield better results.

Share and Connect
Discuss your mistakes with others. Sharing your experiences can not only help you process them but can also inspire and help others who may face similar challenges.

Cultivate Resilience
Mistakes can build resilience. Each error you navigate strengthens your ability to cope with future challenges, making you more adaptable and resourceful.

Conclusion
In summary, mistakes are not the end but rather stepping stones toward growth and improvement. By embracing them with an open mind, reflecting on your experiences, and making necessary adjustments, you can turn setbacks into valuable lessons that propel you forward.

4.3.2. Focus on What You Can Control
In the midst of change, focusing on controllable aspects can reduce stress and help you stay grounded. Strategies include:

Creating a Routine in React

How to Set Achievable Goals

- Practice Mindfulness: Engage in mindfulness techniques to stay present and manage stress.

4.3.3. Build Resilience and Adaptability
Resilience and adaptability are crucial for navigating change. To build these qualities, consider the following:

- Develop Coping Mechanisms: Find healthy ways to cope with stress, such as exercise, meditation, or creative outlets.

- Embrace Flexibility: Be open to new approaches and willing to adapt as circumstances change.

- Stay Positive: Focus on the positive aspects of change and the opportunities it can bring.

4.3.4. Seek Support and Build Connections
A strong support network can help you embrace change and find new opportunities. Strategies to build connections include:

- Reach Out to Trusted Friends and Family: Share your thoughts and feelings with those who can offer encouragement and guidance.

- Join Support Groups: Connect with people who have experienced similar changes to gain insight and advice.

- Build New Relationships: Use change as an opportunity to meet new people and expand your social network.

4.3.5. Reframe Change as a Positive Experience

Reframing your perspective on change can transform it into a positive experience. Strategies for reframing include:

Identifying the Benefits of Change

- Find New Opportunities: Seek out opportunities that arise from change, whether it's a new career path, a chance to learn something new, or a fresh start.

Celebrate Progress| Medium

4.3.6. Embrace Personal Growth and Development

Embracing change can lead to personal growth and development. Here's how to make the most of it:

- Set Personal Goals: Use change as a chance to set new personal goals that align with your evolving values and aspirations.

- Learn New Skills: Explore new skills or hobbies that can contribute to your personal and professional growth.

- **Reflect on Your Journey**: Take time to reflect on how you've grown and what you've learned from your experiences with change.

Conclusion
You can navigate through transitions with confidence and discover new opportunities. Embracing Change and Finding Opportunities is a growth mindset. These strategies can help you make the most of life's changes and lead to a more fulfilling and successful journey.

4.4 Adapting and Evolving in the face of Adversity
Adapting and evolving in the face of adversity requires courage, resilience, and a willingness to embrace change. Whether you're dealing with personal loss or career setbacks, encouragement can help you move forward. Here's a guide to help you find strength and inspiration to adapt and evolve when facing tough times.

1. Acknowledge Your Feelings
It's important to acknowledge the range of emotions that adversity can evoke:

- It's Okay to Feel Overwhelmed: Accept that feeling overwhelmed or scared is natural when facing adversity. Give yourself permission to feel these emotions without judgment.

- Share Your Struggles: Talk to trusted friends, family, or a therapist about what you're going through. Sharing can provide relief and create a sense of connection.

2. Believe in Your Ability to Overcome
Believing in your inner strength and resilience is crucial for adapting to adversity:

- Trust Your Resilience: Remind yourself of past challenges you've overcome. This serves as evidence of your ability to endure and succeed.

- Affirm Your Strengths: Make a list of your strengths and past accomplishments. Use this list to remind yourself of what you're capable of.

How to Navigate Through Adversity and Emerge Stronger

3. Embrace Change and Adaptability
Adapting to change can open doors to growth and new opportunities:

- Be Open to New Possibilities: Even if a situation seems daunting, keep an open mind about what might come out of it. Adaptability is key to finding success in unexpected places.

- Learn from the Experience: Each challenge can teach you something valuable. Consider what lessons you can learn and how they can contribute to your personal growth.

- Welcome Change: Change can be uncomfortable, but it also leads to transformation. By embracing it, you create opportunities for evolution and growth.

4. Take Small Steps Forward
Progress doesn't have to be drastic; small steps can lead to significant change:

- Break Down the Challenge: Divide large challenges into smaller, manageable tasks. This approach makes the process less intimidating and helps maintain momentum.

- Celebrate Small Victories: Recognize and celebrate every step forward, no matter how small. Each achievement is a testament to your adaptability and resilience.

- Keep Moving Forward: Even when progress feels slow, continue to take steps in the right direction. Consistency and persistence are key.

5. Seek Inspiration from Others

Hearing stories of others who have faced and overcome adversity can be inspiring:

- Seek out books, articles and videos that tell stories of people who have triumphed over adversity. These stories can provide valuable insight and encouragement.

- Find the Right Role Model for Yourself. Their guidance can be invaluable.

- Find Supportive Communities. The sense of solidarity can be a powerful motivator.

6. Stay Positive and Hopeful

A positive outlook can make a significant difference in how you approach adversity:

- Focus on the Positives: Identify the positive aspects of your life, even amid adversity. Gratitude can help shift your perspective.

- Keep Hope Alive: Remember that adversity is often temporary. Hope can be a guiding light that helps you stay focused on the brighter days ahead.

- Find Joy in Small Things: Even in difficult times, find joy in simple pleasures—whether it's a sunset, a good book, or a moment with loved ones.

Conclusion

How to Overcome Challenges With determination and support, you can adapt and evolve, no matter what life throws your way.

CHAPTER 5:

After the Rain—Finding Hope and Growth Beyond the Storm

After the storm has passed and the rain has cleared, the landscape of your life may look different, often in unexpected ways. "After the Rain" In this chapter we will discuss the concept of post-traumatic growth, the importance of embracing change.

5.1 The Aftermath of the Storm
The period following a challenging event can be both an end and a beginning. It's a time to reflect on what you've been through and to consider the path ahead. Here's what this phase might look like:

- Mixed Emotions: You might feel relief that the storm has passed, but also experience sadness, loss, or uncertainty about what comes next.

- Assessment and Reflection: This is a time to take stock of what has changed, what you've learned, and what you need to rebuild or redefine.

The aftermath of a storm can reveal new possibilities and opportunities for growth that might not have been plain before.

5.2 Post-Traumatic Growth

- Post-traumatic growth refers to the positive changes that can occur as a result of overcoming adversity. How to Recognize PostTraumatic Growth

- New Perspectives: Adversity can lead to a shift in how you view the world, helping you appreciate the small things and focus on what matters.

- Increased Resilience: Going Through Tough Times Builds Inner Strength

5.2.1 Sharing Adversity with Others
Sharing adversity with others can be a meaningful way to connect, provide support, and foster understanding. Here's a deeper exploration of how to effectively share your experiences of adversity:

1. Identify Your Purpose

- Clarify Your Intentions: Before sharing, think about why you want to share your adversity. Are you seeking support, looking to connect, or hoping to inspire others? Having a clear purpose can guide your conversation.

2. Choose the Right Audience

- Select Trustworthy Individuals: Share your experiences with people you trust and who are likely to respond with empathy and compassion. This could be friends, family, support groups, or a therapist.

- Consider the Context: Some situations may call for a more formal setting (such as a support group), while others may be more suited to casual conversations with friends.

3. Be Honest and Vulnerable

- Share Your Story: Open up about your experiences. Describe the challenges you faced, how they affected you, and what emotions you felt. Authenticity can help others relate to your experience.

- Express Your Feelings: Don't shy away from discussing your emotions. Sharing how adversity impacted your mental and emotional well-being can encourage others to be open as well.

4. Normalize the Experience

- Acknowledge Shared Struggles: Emphasize that everyone faces challenges at different points in life. This helps to normalize adversity, making others feel less isolated in their struggles.

- Encourage Openness: Invite others to share their own experiences if they feel comfortable. This can create a safe space for mutual support.

5. Focus on Resilience and Growth

- Highlight Lessons Learned: Share insights you gained from your experiences. Discuss how you've grown or what coping strategies have helped you navigate adversity.

- Inspire Hope: Remind others that adversity can lead to personal growth and resilience. Sharing positive outcomes can provide encouragement.

6. Be Mindful of Boundaries

- Gauge Comfort Levels: Pay attention to the reactions of the person you're sharing with. If they seem uncomfortable or uninterested, it may be best to change the subject.

- Respect Privacy: Be cautious about sharing details that may involve others without their consent. Focus on your own experience.

7. Encourage Mutual Support

- Offer Help: Let others know that you're there for them if they want to discuss their own challenges. This reciprocity can strengthen relationships.

- Create a Supportive Environment: Foster an atmosphere where people feel safe to share their own adversities without judgment.

8. Follow Up and Stay Connected

- Check In: After sharing, follow up with the person to see how they're feeling. This shows that you care and helps maintain the connection.

- Continue the Dialogue: Keep the lines of communication open for ongoing discussions about challenges, coping strategies, and support.

Conclusion
Sharing adversity can not only lighten your emotional burden but also create connections with others who may be experiencing similar struggles. By being open, honest, and respectful, you can foster a supportive environment that encourages healing, understanding, and resilience. Remember, vulnerability can lead to deeper relationships and a sense of community, making it easier to navigate life's challenges together.

5.3 Embracing Change and New Beginnings
The period after the storm is an opportunity for new beginnings. Here's how you can embrace change and make the most of this time:

- Redefine Your Goals: Use this time to set new personal and professional goals that align with your evolving values and priorities.

Consider the opportunities that have arisen from the changes in your life.

This is a chance to reinvent yourself and explore new aspects of your personality and interests.

5.4 Moving Forward with Purpose
Finding purpose after the rain can guide you toward a more fulfilling future. Here are some steps to help you move forward with a sense of purpose:

Identify Your Passions

- Contribute to Others: Use your experiences to help others who are going through similar challenges. Acts of service can be a source of purpose and meaning.

- Growth Mindset: Continue to seek out opportunities for learning and development.

5.5 Practicing Gratitude and Mindfulness
Gratitude and mindfulness can be powerful tools for appreciating life after the storm:

- Keep a Gratitude Journal: write down things for which you're grateful, helping you focus on the positives in your life.

Mindfulness for the Post-Summer Landscape

- Celebrate Your Progress: Take time to acknowledge how far you've come and celebrate your achievements, no matter how small.

Conclusion
After the rain" represents a period of growth, renewal, and opportunity. While the storms of life can be challenging, they often pave the way for

new beginnings and personal transformation. By embracing change, seeking post-traumatic growth, you can navigate this phase with confidence and hope. Remember that the rain has passed, and now you have the chance to build a brighter and more fulfilling future.

5.6 Post-Adversity Growth: Transforming Challenges into Opportunities

Adversity can be a huge test for our strength and resilience in ways we never anticipated. Yet, from the ashes of difficulty, growth can emerge. What is Post-AdversityGrowth? Let's explore this concept, focusing on the different dimensions of growth that can occur after adversity and how to foster it in your own life.

5.6.1 Dimensions of Post-Adversity Growth

Post-adversity growth, often referred to as post-traumatic growth (PTG), encompasses several dimensions that individuals may experience after facing significant challenges or hardships. Here are the key dimensions of growth that can emerge following adversity:

1. Emotional Growth

- Resilience:Individuals often develop a greater capacity to cope with future challenges, leading to an increased resilience to stress and adversity.

- Emotional Regulation:People may learn to manage their emotions more effectively, leading to improved emotional stability and awareness.

2. Psychological Growth

- Increased Self-Awareness: Adversity can prompt deep self-reflection, leading to a better understanding of one's values, beliefs, strengths, and weaknesses.

- Cognitive Flexibility: Individuals often become better at adapting their thinking and problem-solving approaches, viewing challenges from various perspectives.

3. Social Growth

- Strengthened Relationships: Experiencing adversity can deepen existing relationships and foster new connections, as individuals often seek support and share their experiences with others.

- Empathy and Compassion: Many people develop greater empathy for others who are struggling, leading to a heightened ability to connect with and support those in similar situations.

4. Spiritual Growth

- Reevaluation of Beliefs: Adversity can prompt individuals to reassess their spiritual beliefs and values, leading to a more profound understanding of their purpose in life.

- Sense of Meaning: Many people find a renewed sense of meaning or purpose after adversity, often becoming more committed to causes or practices that resonate with their experiences.

5. Physical Growth

- Health Awareness: Adversity, especially related to health crises, can lead individuals to prioritize their physical well-being, adopting healthier lifestyle choices.

- Stress Management: Individuals may develop better stress management techniques, such as exercise, mindfulness, or relaxation practices, to cope with future challenges.

6. Behavioral Growth

- Increased Proactivity: Individuals may become more proactive in pursuing their goals, taking charge of their lives, and making positive changes.

- Risk-Taking and Exploration: Experiencing adversity can motivate people to take risks, try new things, and seek out new experiences they may have previously avoided.

7. Cognitive Growth

- Enhanced Problem-Solving Skills: People often become more adept at finding solutions to problems and overcoming obstacles, leading to increased confidence in their abilities.

- Broadened Perspective: Adversity can lead to a more nuanced understanding of life, helping individuals appreciate the complexity of experiences and the interconnectedness of human struggles.

Conclusion
Post-adversity growth can manifest in various dimensions, enriching individuals' lives in meaningful ways. By embracing and reflecting on their experiences, individuals can foster growth in emotional, psychological, social, spiritual, physical, behavioral, and cognitive aspects of their lives. Understanding these dimensions can help individuals recognize and nurture their growth journey after facing adversity.

5.6.2 Factors That Contribute to Post-Adversity Growth
Several factors can influence the likelihood and extent of post-adversity growth:

- Building a Family Support System to Help You Through Hard Times

- Resilience and Coping Skills can help you adapt to adversity and find opportunities for growth.

- Mindset and Attitude can be instrumental in promoting post-adversity growth.

- Embracing Change and Seeing It as an Opportunity

5.7 Strategies for Fostering Post-Adversity Growth
1. Reflect on Your Experience

- Take time to reflect on what you've been through and identify the lessons learned from the adversity.Consider how these lessons have influenced your outlook on life and the changes they've brought about.

2. Find Meaning and Purpose

- Discover the meaning and purpose that adversity has given you. This might involve re-evaluating your goals, values, and priorities.

- Explore new avenues for personal anprofessional growth that align with this newfound sense of purpose.

3. Develop Resilience and Coping Skills

- Work on building resilience through mindfulness, stress management, and emotional regulation techniques.

- Seek professional help, such as therapy or counseling, to develop healthy coping mechanisms.

Their story is one of resilience and community. Neighbors and local organizations came together to help them with shelter, food, and clothing. This outpouring of support reminded Tom and Emily of the power of human kindness. As they rebuilt their home, they became active in the community, raising awareness about wildfire safety.

Tom and Emily's journey from loss to rebuilding their lives is a powerful example of how hope and optimism can emerge from the ashes of adversity.

4. Finding a New Path: The Story of Mariam
Mariam worked for a major corporation for over a decade, climbing the career ladder and achieving financial success. But, when her company went through a restructuring, she found herself laid off. The sudden loss of her job left her questioning her identity and future.

Mariam felt lost and unsure of her next steps. But she soon saw the opportunity to pursue her long-held passion for art and design. She enrolled in art classes and began creating and selling her artworkonline. The process of rediscovering her passion brought her immense joy and fulfillment.

Mariam"s journey from corporate executive to artist taught her that adversity can be the catalyst for pursuing dreams. Today, she runs a successful art studio and uses her story to encourage others to embrace change and follow their passions.

Conclusion

Personal stories of finding hope and optimism in the midst of adversity illustrate the power of resilience. We must understand that even in the darkest times, there can be a glimmer of light guiding us toward a brighter future.

5.9 Moving Forward: Embracing the Path Ahead After Adversity**

The Importance of Moving Forward is a way to draw strength from your experiences and embrace the future.

5.9.1 Acknowledging the Journey

Moving forward begins with acknowledging the journey you've been on:

- Reflect on Your Experience: Take time to reflect on what you've gone through, the lessons learned, and the changes it has brought to your life.

- Accept the New Reality: Embrace the reality of what has changed, whether it's a new job, a different routine, or a different set of priorities.

- Recognize Your Strength Acknowledge the resilience and strength it took to overcome adversity. This recognition can fuel your journey forward.

5.9.2 Setting New Goals and Priorities

As you move forward, it's crucial to set new goals and priorities that align with your current values and aspirations:

- Define Your Goals: Think about what you want to achieve in the coming months and years. These goals can be personal, professional, or a mix of both.

- PrioritizeFocus on the things that matter most to you, whether it's spending time with family, or pursuing a new career.

- Create a Plan: Outline the steps you'll take to achieve your goals. Having a plan can provide direction and motivation.

5.9.3 Building a Supportive Environment

Support from others can make a significant difference in your journey forward:

How to Reconnect with Friends and Family during a Life's storm

- Seek Professional Guidance: If needed, consider working with a therapist, counselor, or career coach to help guide your path.

Join groups or communities where you can share your experiences and learn from others who have faced similar challenges.

5.9.4 Developing Resilience and Coping Skills

Resilience is key to moving forward after adversity. Here are some ways to build and maintain resilience:

Mindfulness Techniques to Help You Navigate New Challenges

- Cultivate a Growth Mindset: Embrace the idea that setbacks are opportunities for learning and growth.

Develop Healthy Coping Strategies. Identify activities or practices that help you manage stress and maintain a positive outlook.

5.9.5 Embracing Change and New Opportunities

Moving forward often involves embracing change and exploring neopportunities:

- Be Open to Change: Embrace thechanges that come with overcoming adversity. They can lead to personal growth and new experiences.

Identifying New Career Opportunities

- Take Risks: Don't be afraid to step out of your comfort zone and try something new. Taking risks can lead to unexpected rewards.

5.9.6 Staying Positive and Hopeful
A positive outlook can make the journey ahead more manageable and fulfilling:

- Focus on the Positives: Identify the positive aspects of your life and focus on them, even amid challenges.

- Keep Hope Alive: Remind yourself that adversity is often temporary, and brighter days are ahead.

- Celebrate Small Victories: Acknowledge and celebrate the progress you make, no matter how small. Each step forward is a testament to your resilience.

Conclusion
Moving forward after adversity is a journey that requires strength, resilience, and a positive outlook. To Navigate the Path Forward , remember, each step you take is a stetoward a brighter and more fulfilling future. With determination and the right support, you can move forward and embrace the opportunities that await.

5.10 Encouragement to Keep Pushing Forward and Never Give Up
Life's journey is full of challenges, setbacks, and moments when it feels easier to give up than to push forward. Yet, it's in these times that our strength and determination are tested. How to Keep Moving Forward Despite Obstacle ? Here's a message of encouragement to help you stay resilient and never give up.

drive behind me. He led us and pointed to the site and off he went on his way. It was as if this man was an 'angel-man' sent to rescue me. The covid test/certification was obtained and this paved way for my journey back to my home country. we are never alone and there's always an unseen hand somewhere.

4. The recent experience bordered on a gastro problem and lack of water/tissue in the restroom. I was attending a meeting and no sooner the meeting ended I found myself pressed to use the restroom. I excused myself and approached the restroom located in another building. I eased my self only to discover there was no water nor any tissue (toilet roll) to be used., I stepped into the ante-chamber where the wash hand basin was located and lo and behold I found a single serviette roll beside the wash hand basin. This reinforced my assumption that we are not alone. There's always light in the shadows.

5.10.5 Focus on the Bigger Picture
When you're in the midst of adversity, it's easy to lose sight of the bigger picture. Take a step back and remind yourself of your long-term goals and dreams. Keeping your vision in mind can help you stay focused and motivated, even when the immediate path seems unclear.

5.10.6 Embrace Your Unique Journey
Your journey is yours, and comparing yourself to others can lead to unnecessary stress and self-doubt. Instead, embrace your own path, with all its twists and turns. Recognize that your experiences, no matter how challenging, are shaping you into the person you're meant to be.

5.10.7 Stay Positive and Find Joy in the Journey
A positive attitude can be a powerful tool for overcoming adversity. Find reasons to smile, laugh, and enjoy life, even when things are tough. How to Practice Gratitude

5.10.8 Keep Pushing Forward

Above all, remember that giving up is not an option. You've come this far, and you have the strength to keep going. When you feel like giving up, remind yourself of why you started and the dreams you're working toward. Each day is a new opportunity to make progress and move closer to your goals.

Conclusion

Encouragement to keep pushing forward and never give up is about reminding yourself of your inner strength. Challenges are a natural part of life, but they can also be a source of growth and inspiration. You can keep moving forward with determination and hope, and embracing your unique journey. Remember, the road ahead may be long, but you have everything you need to navigate it. Keep pushing forward, and never give up.

- Relevant: Goals should align with their values and priorities. This ensures they stay motivated and committed.

- Time-bound: Goals should have a deadline to create a sense of urgency and focus.

6.2.4 Embracing Challenges and Change

Setting new goals often involves embracing change and stepping outside of one's comfort zone. Encourage readers to:

- Welcome Challenges: View obstacles as opportunities for growth and learning. Each challenge overcome is a step closer to their goals.

- Adapt to Change: Be flexible and open to new possibilities. Goals may evolve over time, and that's okay.

- Stay Resilient: Persistence is key to achieving goals. When setbacks occur, encourage readers to keep pushing forward.

6.2.5 Celebrating Success and Learning from Failure

Goals are a journey, and along the way, it's essential to celebrate successes and learn from failures:

Celebrating Achievements, This helps maintain motivation and enthusiasm.

- Learn from Failure: Setbacks and failures are part of the journey. The Importance of a Good Reading List

6.2.6 Seeking Support and Accountability

Having a support system can make a significant difference in achieving goals. Encourage readers to:

- Find Partners for their Business

- Join a new commenting forum

- Seek Mentorship: Find mentors or coaches who can provide guidance and advice on reaching their goals.

Conclusion
Setting new goals is a powerful way to take control of one's life and create positive change. Readers can move forward with confidence and purpose, readers can set SMART goals. Be encouraged to aim high, believe in your potential, and never give up on your dreams. The journey toward achieving your goals may be challenging, but the rewards are immeasurable. Keep being inspired to set new goals and strive for greatness. The sky is the limit, and the possibilities are endless.

6.3 Continuous Growth: The Importance of Lifelong Learning and Development

Continuous growth is the ongoing pursuit of learning, development, and self-improvement. It reflects the idea that personal and professional growth is not a destination but a journey. Embracing this mindset can lead to a more fulfilling and successful life. Here's why continuous growth is essential and how it can impact your life.

6.3.1 Staying Relevant in a Changing World
The world is evolving, with technology, industries, and societal norms in a state of flux. Continuous growth ensures that you stay relevant in a changing world:

6.3.2 Adapting to New Challenges :
This flexibility is crucial for personal and professional success.

In a competitive job market, continuous growth helps you stay ahead by acquiring new skills and knowledge.

- Embracing Innovation: Growth-oriented individuals are more open to innovation and change. This mindset can lead to exciting opportunities and career advancements.

6.3.3 Unlocking Personal Fulfillment

Continuous growth can lead to a deeper sense of personal fulfillment and satisfaction:

Lifelong learning allows you to explore new interests This can lead to a richer and more enjoyable life.

- Building Confidence: As you grow and achieve new milestones, your confidence increases. This self-assurance can impact all areas of your life.

Developing a Growth Mindset This mindset can enhance your well-being.

6.3.4 Fostering Resilience and Adaptability

A commitment to continuous growth helps build resilience and adaptability:

- Learning from Setbacks: When you embrace growth, setbacks become valuable learning experiences. This perspective enables you to bounce back from failures and move forward.

This resilience is key to thriving in the face of challenges

Continuous growth equips you with the skills and mindset to adapt to life's inevitable changes.

6.3.5 Promoting Career Advancement

Continuous growth is crucial for career advancement and success:

Lifelong learning lets you get new skills and knowledge that can open doors to new career opportunities.

Developing a Growth Mindset

- Advancing in Your Career: Employers value individuals who show a commitment to growth. Continuous growth can lead to promotions, career shifts, and increased job satisfaction.

6.3.6 Building Stronger Relationships
Continuous growth also plays a role in building stronger relationships with others:

6.3.7 The Importance of Mentoring
Mentoring is a powerful and transformative process that can significantly impact both the mentor and the mentee. Here are several key reasons why mentoring is important:

1. Knowledge Transfer

- Experience Sharing: Mentors share their knowledge, skills, and experiences, providing mentees with valuable insights that can accelerate their learning and professional development.

- Practical Guidance: Mentees benefit from practical advice and strategies that can help them navigate challenges and make informed decisions.

2. Personal Development

- Skill Enhancement: Mentoring helps mentees develop both hard and soft skills, fostering competencies such as communication, problem-solving, and critical thinking.

- Self-Confidence: Support and encouragement from a mentor can boost a mentee's self-esteem and confidence, empowering them to take on new challenges.

3. Networking Opportunities

- Connections: Mentors often introduce mentees to their professional networks, opening doors to new opportunities, collaborations, and resources.

- Visibility: Being associated with a mentor can enhance a mentee's visibility in their field, helping them build relationships with influential individuals.

4. Career Advancement

- Guidance on Career Paths: Mentors can provide insights into potential career trajectories, helping mentees identify goals and develop plans to achieve them.

- Navigating Challenges: Mentors can offer support in overcoming obstacles and navigating workplace dynamics, increasing the likelihood of career advancement.

5. Emotional Support

- Safe Space for Discussion: Mentors provide a trusted environment where mentees can openly discuss concerns, fears, and aspirations.

- Encouragement: A mentor's encouragement can be invaluable during challenging times, helping mentees maintain motivation and focus.

6. Diversity and Inclusion

- Broaden Perspectives: Mentoring relationships can foster diversity by connecting individuals from different backgrounds, cultures, and experiences. This diversity enriches the mentoring experience for both parties.

- Promoting Inclusion: Mentors can advocate for underrepresented individuals in their fields, helping to create a more inclusive environment.

7. Leadership Development

- Skill Building for Mentors: Mentoring develops leadership skills for mentors as they learn to guide, motivate, and inspire others.

- Succession Planning: Effective mentoring helps cultivate the next generation of leaders within an organization or community.

8. Fostering Lifelong Learning

- Cultivating Curiosity: Mentoring encourages a culture of continuous learning, inspiring both mentors and mentees to seek knowledge and growth throughout their careers.

- Feedback Loops: Regular interactions between mentors and mentees facilitate constructive feedback, enhancing the learning experience.

9. Community Building

- Strengthening Relationships: Mentoring fosters a sense of belonging and community, both within organizations and in larger professional networks.

- Shared Values: Mentoring relationships often promote shared values and goals, contributing to a positive organizational culture.

Conclusion

Mentoring is a mutually beneficial relationship that can lead to significant personal and professional growth for both the mentor and mentee. By facilitating knowledge transfer, emotional support, and networking opportunities, mentoring plays a crucial role in fostering the development of individuals and strengthening communities. Whether in a professional setting, educational environment, or personal life, the impact of mentoring can be profound and far-reaching.

Conclusion

Continuous growth is a vital part of a fulfilling and successful life. Adaptability is the key to a successful career. Adaptability is a growth mindset and committing to lifelong learning. Remember, growth is a journey without an end, and every step you take contributes to your development. Keep learning, keep growing, and never stop striving for a better version of yourself.

CHAPTER 7:
Empowering Others

Empowering others is not just an act of kindness; it is a noble calling that can create ripples of change in our communities and beyond. In this chapter, I explore the profound impact we can have when we lift others up, providing support and encouragement as they navigate their own storms. Through personal experiences, strategies, and reflections, I aim to inspire you to become a beacon of hope for those around you.

7.1 The Ripple Effect of Empowerment
When we empower others, we create a chain reaction of positivity and strength. I recall a time when a close friend of mine was going through a difficult period. He felt overwhelmed by the pressures of work and family obligations, and his spirit was dimmed. Sensing his struggle, I reached out to offer my support. I listened to his concerns, validated his feelings, and encouraged him to take time for himself.

In that moment, I realized how powerful it is to simply be present for someone in need. My support not only helped him regain his footing but also inspired him to pay it forward. He began to extend his hand to others who were struggling, creating a cycle of empowerment that spread through our circle of friends. This experience illuminated the truth that when we lift others, we elevate ourselves in the process.

7.2 The Art of Active Listening
One of the most effective ways to empower others is through active listening. Often, people just need someone to hear them without judgment. By creating a safe space for sharing, we invite others to express their fears, dreams, and challenges.

During a particularly challenging time for my community, I organized a support group where individuals could come together to share their stories and experiences . As I listened to their struggles, I realized that my role was not to provide solutions but to simply validate their emotions. This act of listening fostered a sense of belonging and community, encouraging participants to support one another and to form a community Group.

In your own life, practice active listening by giving your full attention to those who seek your support. Ask open-ended questions, refrain from interrupting, and reflect back what you hear. This approach not only empowers others but also strengthens your relationships.

7.3 Offering Practical Support
Empowerment often involves providing practical support that enables others to take action. This could be helping someone with their resume, offering to babysit while a friend attends a job interview, or sharing resources to help them navigate a difficult situation.

I remember a colleague who was struggling to balance her workload with her responsibilities at home. Recognizing her stress, I offered to assist with some of her tasks at work. By alleviating some of her burdens, she was able to focus on her family and take the necessary steps to achieve a healthier work-life balance.

Consider the skills and resources you possess that could benefit those around you. By offering tangible support, you empower others to regain control over their circumstances and thrive.

7.4 Inspiring Through Example

One of the most powerful ways to empower others is to lead by example. When we embody resilience, positivity, and a willingness to overcome challenges, we inspire those around us to do the same.

I have always believed in the importance of sharing my own journey, including the struggles I have faced and the lessons I have learned. By being transparent about my experiences, I hope to demonstrate that vulnerability is not a weakness but a strength. When others see that it is possible to rise from adversity, they are more likely to find the courage to face their own challenges.

Share your stories, celebrate your triumphs, and acknowledge your setbacks. Your journey can serve as a source of inspiration for others navigating their own storms.

7.5 Celebrating the Success of Others

Empowerment is not just about lifting others during their struggles; it is also about celebrating their successes. When someone achieves a goal, no matter how small, acknowledge their efforts and cheer them on.

I recall attending a small gathering where a friend shared her recent promotion at work. Instead of merely congratulating her, I took the time to highlight the hard work and dedication that led her to this achievement. The joy in her eyes as she felt seen and appreciated was a reminder of the importance of recognizing the efforts of those around us.

Make it a practice to celebrate the successes of others. By doing so, you reinforce their self-worth and encourage them to continue pursuing their dreams.

7.6 Conclusion: A Call to Action

As we conclude this chapter, I invite you to reflect on the ways you can empower those around you. Each of us has the capacity to be a source of strength and hope in someone else's life. Whether through active listening, offering practical support, leading by example, or celebrating the successes of others, you can make a meaningful difference.

Empowering others is a celebration of service, a testament to the interconnectedness of our journeys. As you embrace this calling, remember that when we uplift one another, we create a world where everyone has the opportunity to thrive. Let us be beacons of hope, lighting the way through the storms of life, together.

CHAPTER 8:
The Gift of Adversity

Adversity can be one of life's most challenging experiences, yet it often bears gifts that we cannot see until we emerge on the other side. In this chapter, I invite you to explore the profound lessons that adversity can teach us, the resilience it can foster, and the unexpected blessings that may arise from our struggles.

8.1 Embracing the Storm

I remember a particularly tumultuous period in my life when everything seemed to crumble around me. I had just lost my job unexpectedly, and the weight of uncertainty loomed over me like a dark cloud. In the initial shock, I felt defeated and overwhelmed, questioning my worth and future. However, as days turned into weeks, I began to realize that this adversity was pushing me toward self-discovery in ways I never anticipated.

In the quiet moments of reflection, I unearthed a passion for writing that had long been dormant. What began as a coping mechanism soon transformed into a powerful outlet for my emotions. I discovered the cathartic (providing psychological relief) release that came from putting pen to paper, and in doing so, I found clarity and purpose. This experience taught me that sometimes, we must be stripped of our comforts to rediscover our true selves.

8.2 Lessons in Resilience

Adversity is a master teacher, imparting lessons that foster resilience. The challenges we face often require us to dig deep within ourselves. Each obstacle presents an opportunity to rise stronger, and with every setback, we cultivate the grit that propels us forward.

Reflecting on my journey, I recall a time when I faced significant health challenges. I had a 6 hour back surgery. The physical pain was excruciating, but it was the emotional and mental turmoil that truly tested my spirit. I learned to lean on my support system, to ask for help, and to find strength in vulnerability. This experience taught me that resilience is not about never falling; it's about having the courage to rise each time we do.

8.3 Finding Silver Linings

As I navigated the storms of life, I began to notice the silver linings that often accompany adversity. During my job loss, I had the opportunity to reconnect with old friends and family, strengthening bonds that had faded over time. These relationships provided a network of support that was invaluable, reminding me that I was never truly alone.

Moreover, facing health challenges opened my eyes to the fragility of life and the importance of self-care. I learned to prioritize my well-being, embracing practices that nourished my mind, body, and spirit. Adversity can be a wake-up call, urging us to reassess our priorities and make changes that lead to a more fulfilling life.

8.4 The Transformative Power of Perspective

Perhaps the greatest gift of adversity is the shift in perspective it can bring. When we are confronted with challenges, we often gain clarity about what truly matters. The things that once seemed significant become trivial in the face of hardship. We learn to cherish the simple joys—a warm cup of coffee, a hug from a loved one, or a moment of laughter.

In sharing my experiences, I hope to inspire you to embrace your adversities as opportunities for growth. Each challenge you face is a stepping stone on your journey, shaping you into the person you are meant to be. The lessons learned in the shadows can illuminate the path ahead, guiding you toward a brighter future.

8.5 Conclusion: A Tribute to Strength

In conclusion, let us celebrate the transformative power of adversity. It is often through our darkest moments that we unearth our greatest strengths. Each trial we endure is a chapter in our story, contributing to the rich tapestry of our lives. As we honor the lessons and blessings that arise from adversity, may we find solace in the knowledge that we are resilient, capable of weathering any storm that comes our way.

As you reflect on your own life, I encourage you to seek the gifts hidden within your challenges. Embrace the journey, for it is in the struggle that we discover our true potential and the brilliance that lies within us all. Together, let us rise, stronger and wiser, ready to face whatever storms may come.

CHAPTER 9:
The Dawn of Hope

As we come to the end of this journey together, I want to leave you with a powerful reminder: every storm eventually gives way to the dawn of hope. No matter how dark the clouds may seem, there always lies the promise of brighter days ahead. In this final chapter, I share a message of optimism, faith, and strength for the future—encouragement for those of you navigating your own storms.

9.1 Embracing the Journey
Life is a series of ebbs and flows, of challenges followed by moments of triumph. Each storm we encounter is a part of our unique journey, shaping us into who we are meant to be. It is essential to embrace the journey, understanding that the difficulties we face are often the catalysts for our growth.

I recall a particularly challenging time when I felt lost and unsure of my path. It was during this period that I discovered the importance of patience and self-compassion. I learned to honor my feelings, recognizing that it was okay to seek solace in the storms. Sometimes, just allowing ourselves to be vulnerable is the first step toward healing.

Remember, it's not about how quickly you get through the storm, but about what you learn along the way. Embrace the process, and trust that each experience contributes to your story.

9.2 Cultivating a Mindset of Hope

Hope is a powerful force that can lift us from our darkest moments. It is the glimmer of light that shines through the cracks of despair, reminding us that change is possible. Cultivating a mindset of hope involves consciously choosing to focus on possibilities rather than limitations.

In my own life, I have found that practicing gratitude has been instrumental in nurturing this hopeful mindset. Each day, I take a moment to reflect on the blessings in my life, no matter how small. This practice allows me to shift my perspective, enabling me to see the beauty even in difficult times.

I encourage you to adopt a similar practice. Each morning, set aside a few moments to acknowledge the things you are grateful for. This simple act can serve as a powerful reminder that, despite the storms, there is always something to be hopeful about.

9.3 The Strength of Community

As we navigate our storms, it's vital to remember that we are not alone. The strength of community can be a lifeline during our darkest hours. Surrounding ourselves with supportive individuals who lift us up can make all the difference in our journey.

I have been fortunate to have a network of friends and mentors who have offered unwavering support during my challenges. Their encouragement reminded me that I was not facing my storms in isolation. Instead, we were in this together, united in our struggles and triumphs.

As you face your own storms, reach out to those around you. Lean on your community, share your experiences, and allow others to be a source of strength for you. Together, we can weather any storm.

9.4 The Power of Resilience

Resilience is the ability to bounce back from adversity, and it is a skill that can be cultivated over time. Life will undoubtedly present challenges, but it is how we respond to those challenges that defines our journey.

Reflecting on my past adversities, I recognize how each one has contributed to my resilience. The moments when I thought I would break ultimately became the moments that strengthened my resolve. I learned to adapt, to find creative solutions, and to hold onto hope even in the face of uncertainty.

To build your own resilience, embrace the challenges you encounter. Rather than viewing them as setbacks, see them as opportunities to grow stronger and wiser. You have the power to transform your struggles into stepping stones toward a brighter future.

9.5 A Call to Keep Moving Forward

As we conclude this chapter and our journey together, I leave you with this call to action: keep moving forward. Life is a continuous journey, and while storms may come and go, the dawn of hope is always on the horizon.

Embrace each day as a new opportunity to take a step toward your dreams, to lift others, and to cultivate hope within yourself. Remember that you are equipped with the strength, resilience, and courage to face whatever challenges may arise.

You are not defined by your storms; you are defined by how you rise from them. Trust in your ability to navigate the journey ahead, knowing that bright skies are always within reach.

9.6 Conclusion: Hope is Always Ahead

In closing, I want to remind you that hope is not a distant dream; it is a reality waiting to be embraced. As you move through life, carry the message of optimism and faith in your heart. Every dawn brings new possibilities, and every storm eventually gives way to the light of a new day.

Let this be your mantra: "Bright skies are always ahead." Whenever you face challenges, hold onto this truth, and let it guide you through the storms of life. Together, let us step forward into the light, empowered by hope and ready to create a future filled with promise and possibility.

CHAPTER 10:

Recap of Key Themes and Takeaways from "Bright Skies Ahead: Overcoming Life's Storms"

As we come to the end of "Bright Skies Ahead: Overcoming Life's storms," let's recap the key themes and takeaways from the book. This journey has been about finding hope, strength, and resilience during life's most challenging moments. By exploring strategies and stories that inspire us to push through adversity, we can leave with a sense of empowerment.

10.1 Understanding the Storms
In the early chapters, we delved into the various storms that life can bring. W explored how storms can leave us feeling lost, afraid, and overwhelmed. We examined common reactions to these challenges, such as fear, denial, anger, sadness, and withdrawal.

10.2 Preparing for the Storms
1.Preparation is crucial when navigating life's storms. Social Networking: How to Build a Strong Community Through these practices, we can develop a solid foundation. By fostering a culture of service and supporting others, we create a network of strength that benefits everyone.

10.3 Navigating Through the Storms

These stories offer valuable lessons about resilience, determination, and the power of community. I highlighted key strategies for finding support during difficult times. We encourage readers to seek help when needed.

10.4 Embracing Change and Growth

Change is inevitable, but it can also be an opportunity for growth and transformation. We explored how to embrace change and find opportunities for growth in the midst of adversity. By adapting to new circumstances and evolving, we can emerge stronger and more resilient. This section encouraged readers to embrace change with an open mind and see it as a pathway to personal development.

10.5 After the Rain

In the final chapters, we discussed the concept of post-adversity growth and shared personal stories of hope and optimism. We explored how individuals found light after the storm and rebuilt their lives. These stories serve as a testament to the human spirit's resilience and the possibility of a brighter future. We encouraged readers to keep pushing forward, no matter how challenging the journey may be.

10.6 The Sky is the Limit

Throughout the book, the theme 'The Sky is the Limit' underscored the idea that there are no boundaries to what we can achieve. By setting new goals and growing, we can reach new heights and unlock our full potential. We encouraged readers to dream big, set SMART goals, and stay committed to their journey of growth.

10.7 Empowering Others

Empowering others is not just an act of kindness; it is a noble calling that can create ripples of change in our communities and beyond. In this chapter, I explore the profound impact we can have when we lift others up, providing support and encouragement as they navigate their own storms. Through personal experiences, strategies, and reflections, I aim to inspire you to become a beacon of hope for those around you.

10.8 The Gift Of Adversity
Adversity can be one of life's most challenging experiences, yet it often bears gifts that we cannot see until we emerge on the other side. In this chapter, I invite you to explore the profound lessons that adversity can teach us, the resilience it can foster, and the unexpected blessings that may arise from our struggles.

10.9 The Dawn of Hope
As we come to the end of this journey together, I want to leave you with a powerful reminder: every storm eventually gives way to the dawn of hope. No matter how dark the clouds may seem, there always lies the promise of brighter days ahead. In this final chapter, I share a message of optimism, faith, and strength for the future—encouragement for those of you navigating your own storms.

CHAPTER 11"
Final Thoughts

As we conclude, remember that life will bring storms, but you have the strength and courage to overcome them. To Survive During Hard Times, Embrace challenges, seek support from others, and never stop striving for personal growth.

Thank you for joining me on this journey. "Bright Skies Ahead: Overcoming Life's Storms" has provided you with the inspiration and tools to face your own storms. Remember, the sky is the limit, and you are capable of achieving incredible things. Keep pushing forward, and always believe in the brightness that lies ahead.

11.1 Encouragement to Embrace the Journey of Overcoming Life's Storms

It's not always an easy path, but it's onthat leads to growth, transformation, and a deeper understanding of yourself. Here's some encouragement to help you embrace this journey and find the strength to navigate through adversity.

11.1.1 Acknowledge the Storm
The first step9 in overcoming life's storms is acknowledging their presence. This means facing reality and accepting that challenges are a natural part of life. By recognizing the storm, you take the first step toward finding a

way through it. Remember, denial only delays the healing process, while acceptance allows you to focus on solutions.

11.1.2 Embrace the Process of Growth
Every storm has the potential to help you grow, even if it doesn't seem like it at the time. Embrace the process of growth by:

- Learning from Experience: Each challenge offers valuable lessons. Take time to reflect on what you're learning about yourself and the world around you.

- Finding New Strengths: Storms often reveal strengths you didn't know you had. Embrace the journey to discover hidden talents and abilities.

- Developing Resilience: The ability to bounce back from setbacks is a powerful skill. Each storm you weather makes you more resilient for the future.

11.1.3 Seek Support from Others
Overcoming life's storms doesn't mean you have to do it alone. Seek support from friends, family, and community. Sharing your journey with others can provide comfort, encouragement, and practical advice. It's a reminder that you're not alone, and there are people who care about your well-being.

11.1.4 Stay Positive and Find Joy
It's easy to feel overwhelmed by life's storms, but finding joy in the midst of adversity is a powerful way to stay positive. Look for the small moments that bring you happiness—a beautiful sunset, a kind word from a friend, or a simple act of kindness. These moments can brighten even the darkest days and remind you that there's always something to be grateful for.

11.1.5 Keep Moving Forward

The journey through a storm can be long and challenging, but the key is to keep moving forward. Set small, achievable goals, and celebrate your progress along the way. Each step you take brings you closer to brighter skies. Remember, persistence is the key to overcoming adversity.

11.1.6 Trust in the Journey

Trust that the journey of overcoming life's storms is leading you to a better place. Even when the path is unclear, have faith that you're moving toward growth and transformation. Embrace the uncertainty, knowing that every storm has an end, and you'll emerge stronger on the other side.

Conclusion

Embracing the journey of overcoming life's storms is about finding strength in the face of adversity. Acknowledge the storm, embrace the process of growth, seek support from others, find joy, keep moving forward, and trust in the journey. Remember, you're not alone, and there's always hope for brighter days ahead.

You have the resilience, courage, and determination to overcome anything that comes your way. Embrace the journey, and never sto believing in your own strength. The sky may be stormy now, but the sun will shine again, and you'll be there to enjoy its warmth. Keep going—you've got this.

11.2 Message of Hope and Positivity for the Future

As we journey through life, it's natural to encounter challenges and uncertainties. But, it's important to remember that no matter how daunting the storms may seem, they pass, and brighter days lie ahead. Here's a message of hope and positivity to inspire you as you look toward the future.

11.2.1 Hope Is a Beacon of Light

Hope is the light that guides us through the darkest times. It serves as a reminder that even when everything seems bleak, there's always a reason to believe in a better tomorrow. Hope gives us the strength to keep moving forward, even when the path is uncertain. Let hope be your guiding light as you navigate the ups and downs of life.

11.2.2 Embrace the Power of Positivity

Positivity is a powerful force that can transform your outlook and change the course of your journey. When you focus on the positive aspects of life, you invite more joy and optimism into your world. Positivity is not ignoring challenges Embrace positivity, and you'll find that it has the power to uplift and inspire you.

11.2.3 Believe in Your Potential

You have incredible potential within you, waiting to be unlocked. Believe in your abilities and know that you are capable of achieving great things. Each step you take toward your goals, no matter how small, isa step toward realizing your full potential. Trust in your journey and have faith in your capacity to overcome any obstacles that come your way.

11.2.4 Celebrate the Small Victories

The journey to a brighter future is made up of many small victories. Celebrate each achievement, no matter how minor it may seem. These moments of success remind you that progress is happening and that you're moving in the right direction. By recognizing and celebrating the small victories, you create a positive momentum that propels you forward.

11.2.5 Surround Yourself with Support

You don't have to face the future alone. Surround yourself with supportive people who believe in you and your dreams. The presence of friends, family, and mentors can make a world of difference during challenging times. Lean on them for encouragement and guidance, and offer the same support in return. Together, you can create a network of positivity and hope that strengthens you on your journey.

11.2.6 Keep Moving Forward
No matter what challenges you face, keep moving forward. Progress might be slow, and setbacks might occur, but each day brings new opportunities for growth and change. Keep your eyes on the future, and take one step at a time. Remember, the journey may be long, but the destination is worth it.

11.2.7 The Future Is Bright
As you look toward the future, know that it's filled with endless possibilities. You have the power to shape your destiny and create the life you desire. The road ahead may be filled with twists and turns, but it's also filled with new experiences, opportunities, and moments of joy. Embrace the journey with hope and positivity, and you'll find that the future is brighter than you could have ever imagined.

11.2.8 The Dawn Of Hope
Let this be your mantra: "Bright skies are always ahead." Whenever you face challenges, hold onto this truth, and let it guide you through the storms of life. Together, let us step forward into the light, empowered by hope and ready to create a future filled with promise and possibility.

Conclusion
In the end, hope and positivity are the keys to a fulfilling and meaningful life. They give you the strength to face challenges, the courage to pursue your dreams, and the resilience to keep going when times are tough. 5 Ways to Embrace Positivity The future is yours to create, and it's filled with bright skies ahead.

APPENDICES

Appendices for "Bright Skies Ahead: Overcoming Life's Storms"

The appendices in this book serve as extra resources and tools to support readers on their journey of overcoming life's storms. They offer practical advice, checklists, more readings, and other helpful materials. Here are the appendices:

Appendix A: Coping Tools and Techniques
This appendix provides a comprehensive list of coping tools and techniques discussed in the book. It includes:

- Mindfulness Exercises: Simple mindfulness practices to help readers stay grounded during stressful times.

- Breathing Techniques Instructions for deep breathing and relaxation exercises.

Journaling for Personal Growth

- Physical Activities: A list of exercises and activities that can help reduce stress and improve mood.

Mindfulness Exercises

Mindfulness exercises can be a powerful way to manage stress, improve focus, and cultivate a greater sense of well-being. By grounding yourself in the present moment, you can reduce anxiety and gain a clearer perspective on the challenges you face. Here are some mindfulness exercises to help you practice staying present and centered:

Breathing Exercises
Deep Breathing:

- Find a quiet place to sit or lie down.

- Close your eyes and take a deep breath in through your nose, counting to four.

- Hold your breath for a count of four, then exhale through your mouth for another count of four.

- Repeat this process several times, focusing on the sensation of your breath entering and leaving your body.

Alternate Nostril Breathing:

- Sit and use your right thumb to close your right nostril.

- Inhale through your left nostril, then close it with your right ring finger.

- Release your right nostril and exhale through it.

- Inhale through your right nostril, close it, then release your left nostril to exhale.

- Continue this pattern for a few cycles, focusing on your breathing rhythm.

Body Scan Meditation
Full Body Scan:

- Lie down or sit in a comfortable position, closing your eyes.

- Start by focusing on your toes. Notice any sensations or tension, and relax them.

- move your focus up through your body—feet, legs, torso, arms, neck, and head.

- Take time at each point to notice and release any tension, focusing on your breath as you progress through the scan.

Progressive Muscle Relaxation:

- While lying down, tense the muscles in your toes for a few seconds, then relax them.

- Move to the calves, then thighs, and continue upward, tensing and then relaxing each muscle group.

- This exercise can help you become more aware of your body's sensations and release tension.

Mindful Eating
Sensory Awareness:

- Choose a small piece of food, such as a raisin or a piece of chocolate.

- Before eating, examine it, noting its texture, color, and aroma.

- As you eat, focus on the sensations—how it feels in your mouth, the taste, and the texture.

- Eat and, savoring each bite and staying present with the experience.

Mindful Movement
Walking Meditation:

- Find a quiet place to walk, either indoors or outdoors.

- Walk, paying attention to each step. Notice the sensation of your feet touching the ground, the movement of your legs, and the rhythm of your breathing.

- As you walk, focus on your surroundings—sounds, sights, and smells—while maintaining a steady pace.

Yoga and Stretching:

- Engage in gentle yoga or stretching exercises. Focus on your breathing and the sensations in your body as you move through each pose or stretch.

- Allow yourself to be present during the practice, letting go of distractions and concentrating on the flow of movement.

Guided Meditation and Visualization
Guided Meditation:

- Listen to a guided meditation that leads you through a calming journey. This can be a nature scene, a place of tranquility, or an experience of relaxation.

- Follow the guide's instructions, focusing on your breathing and the imagery provided.

Visualization:

- Sit or lie down in a comfortable position, closing your eyes.

- Imagine a peaceful scene—a beach, a forest, or a mountaintop. Visualize the details, including the sights, sounds, and smells.

- Spend a few minutes in this peaceful place, allowing your mind to relax and your stress to melt away.

These mindfulness exercises can help you stay grounded, reduce stress, and develop a greater sense of awareness in your daily life. Practice them to build a mindfulness habit and improve your well-being.

Breathing Techniques for Relaxation and Stress Relief
Breathing techniques are powerful tools for relaxation, stress relief, and mindfulness. By focusing on your breath, you can calm your mind, lower your stress levels, and gain better control over your emotions. Here are some effective breathing techniques to help you manage stress and maintain a sense of calm:

Diaphragmatic Breathing (Belly Breathing)
Diaphragmatic breathing involves engaging the diaphragm to take deep, full breaths. It helps reduce stress and promotes relaxation.

1. Get Comfortable: Sit or lie down in a relaxed position.

2. Place Your Hands: Rest one hand on your chest and the other on your abdomen.

3. Inhale: Breathe in through your nose, allowing your abdomen to rise while keeping your chest still.

4. Exhale: Release your breath through your mouth, feeling your abdomen fall as you exhale.

5. Repeat: Continue this process for several cycles, focusing on the rise and fall of your abdomen.

Box Breathing (Four-Square Breathing)
Box breathing is a simple technique that involves equalizing the inhale, hold, exhale, and hold times. It's great for calming anxiety and reducing stress.

1. Find a Quiet Space: Sit or stand.

2. Inhale: Breathe in through your nose for a count of four.

3. Hold: Hold your breath for a count of four.

4. Exhale: release your breath through your mouth for a count of four.

5. Hold: Hold again for a count of fur.

6. Repeat: Continue for several cycles, focusing on the rhythm and counting.

4-7-8 Breathing

This breathing technique is designed to promote relaxation and help with sleep. It involves a pattern of inhaling, holding, and exhaling.

1. Get Comfortable: Sit or lie down in a quiet space.

2. Inhale: Breathe in through your nose for a count of four.

3. Hold: Hold your breath for a count of seven.

4. Exhale: Exhale through your mouth for a count of eight.

5. Repeat: Continue for several cycles, maintaining a slow and steady pace.

Alternate Nostril Breathing

Alternate nostril breathing is a traditional yoga technique that helps balance the body and mind.

1. Sit: Find a relaxed seating position.

2. Close One Nostril: Use your thumb to close your right nostril.

3. Inhale: Breathe in through your left nostril, then close it with your ring finger.

4. Exhale: Release your thumb and exhale through the right nostril.

5. Alternate: Now inhale through your right nostril, then close it and release your ring finger to exhale through the left nostril.

6. Repeat: Continue this pattern for several cycles, focusing on the flow of breath and the alternating pattern.

Lion's Breath

Lion's breath is a fun and energizing breathing technique that can release tension and boost energy.

1. Sit in a Comfortable Position: You can sit on your knees or in a chair.

2. Inhale: Breathe in through your nose, filling your lungs.

3. Exhale with Force: Open your mouth wide, stick out your tongue, and exhale with a forceful "ha" sound.

4. Add a Gesture: For added effect, open your eyes wide and spread your fingers as you exhale.

5. Repeat: Perform a few cycles, allowing yourself to let go of stress and tension.

These breathing techniques can be practiced or in combination, depending on your needs and comfort level. They are versatile tools for managing stress, promoting relaxation, and enhancing mindfulness. Incorporate them into your daily routine to experience their benefits.

Journaling Techniques for Self-Reflection and Personal Growth
Journaling can be a powerful tool for self-reflection, stress relief, and personal growth. It allows you to explore your thoughts, emotions, and experiences in a structured way, helping you gain clarity and insight. Here are several journaling techniques you can use to navigate life'storms and foster personal development.

Gratitude Journaling
Gratitude journaling involves focusing on the positive aspects of your life. It can boost your mood, increase optimism, and promote a greater sense of well-being.

- Daily Gratitude List: Write down three things you're grateful for each day. This simple practice can shift your mindset towards positivity.

- Gratitude Prompts: Use prompts to explore gratitude in more depth. Fr example, "Describe a person who has made a positive impact on your life."

- Thankfulness Letters: Write a letter to someone you're thankful for, expressing your appreciation.

Reflective Journaling
What is Reflective Journaling?

- Stream of Consciousness: Write without filtering your thoughts. This technique allows you to express yourself and uncover underlying emotions.

- Reflect on Events: Choose an event or experience and explore it in detail. Describe what happened, how you felt, and what you learned.

- Identify Patterns: Look for recurring themes or patterns in your life. This can help you identify areas for growth and development.

Goal-Setting Journaling
Goal-setting journaling is about defining your goals and tracking your progress toward achieving them.

Emotion-Focused Journaling
Emotion-focused journaling allows you to explore your emotions and fnd healthy ways to process them.

- Emotion Identification: Write about a specific emotion you're feeling. Describe what triggered it and how it manifests in your body.

- Coping Strategies: Explore different coping strategies for managing challenging emotions. Write about what has worked for you in the past.

Writing about an Emotional Experience This technique can help release pent-up emotions and promote healing.

Future Visualization
What is Future Visualization?

- Visualize Success: Write about your ideal future, describing what success looks like for you. Include details about your career, relationships,and personal goals.

- Create a Vision Board: Use words and images to create a visual representation of your future goals. This can serve as a source of inspiration.

- Letter to Your Future Self: Write a letter to your future self, outlining your hopes and dreams. Include advice and encouragement for the journey ahead.

Guided Journaling
Guided journaling involves using prompts and questions to guide yur writing.

- Prompted Journaling: Use prompts or questions to spark ideas and guide your journaling session. For example, "What does success mean to you?" or "Describe a moment of personal growth."

Journaling with a Theme
Journaling Techniques for Self-Care

Physical Activities for Stress Relief and Well-Being
Physical activities can be an excellent way to relieve stress, improve mood, and maintain omit health. Regular exercise not only benefits your physical body but also has a profound impact on your mental and emotional well-being. Here are some physical activities you can incorporate into your routine to help overcome life's storms.

Aerobic Exercises

Aerobic exercises, also known as cardio, can increase your heart rate, improve circulation, and boost energy levels. They are effective for reducing stress and anxiety.

- Walking or Jogging: Take a brisk walk or go for a light jog in a park or along a scenic route. This low-impact exercise is accessible to most people.

- Cycling: Ride a bicycle outdoors or use a stationary bike. Cycling is a great way to get a full-body workout and explore your surroundings.

- Swimming: Swim laps in a pool or enjoy a swim in a lake or ocean. Swimming provides a low-impact workout and can be relaxing.

Strength Training

Strength training involves using resistance to build muscle and increase strength. It can boost confidence and promote a sense of accomplishment.

- Bodyweight Exercises: Perform exercises like push-ups, squats, lunges, and planks. These need no equipment and can be done anywhere.

- Weightlifting: Use dumbbells, barbells, or resistance bands to build muscle. Start with lighter weights and increase the intensity.

How to Train Your Body for Fitness This type of training can improve omit strength and functionality.

Flexibility and Balance Exercises

How to Improve Flexibility and Balance Exercises

- Yoga: Practice yoga poses to enhance flexibility, balance, and mindfulness. Yoga combines physical movement with breathing exercises and meditation.

- Stretching: Perform static and dynamic stretches to improve flexibility. Stretch major muscle groups and focus on areas that tend to hold tension.

- Pilates: Engage in Pilates exercises to improve core strength, balance, and flexibility. Pilates oft uses controlled movements to strengthen the body.

Mind-Body Activities
Mind-body activities combine physical movement with mindfulness and relaxation techniques. They can be effective for stress relief and mental clarity.

- Tai Chi: Practice Tai Chi, a gentle form of martial arts that focuses on slow, flowing movements. Tai Chi can improve balance and reduce stress.

Recreational Activities
Recreational activities can be a fun and engaging way to stay active while reducing stress.

- Team Sports: Join a local sports team or play casual games with friends. Sports like soccer, basketball, or volleyball can foster teamwork and social connections.

- Dancing: Take a dance class or dance at home. Dancing is a joyful way to get exercise and express yourself.

- Outdoor Activities: Go hiking, rock climbing, or kayaking. Outdoor activities allow you to connect with nature and challenge yourself.

Incorporating Physical Activities into Your Routine
To reap the benefits of physical activities, consider the following tips:

- Find Activities You Enjoy: Choose activities that you find enjoyable and motivating. This will make it easier to stay consistent.

- Set Realistic Goals: Start with manageable goals and increase the intensity and duration of your workouts.

- Create a Routine: Establish a regular exercise routine that fits into your schedule. Consistency is key to achieving lasting benefits.

- Mix It Up: Incorporate a variety of activities to keep things interesting and engage different muscle groups.

- Stay Hydrated and Rested: Drink plenty of water and get enough rest to support your physical activities and omit well-being.

These physical activities can help you manage stress, boost energy, improve your mood. Experiment with different types of exercises to find what works best for you, and enjoy the positive impact they have on your life.

Appendix B: Resources for Mental Health and Support
A compilation of resources for readers seeking more support or professional help, including:

- Mental Health Hotlines: A list of crisis hotlines and emergency contacts by region or country.

- Therapists and Counselors: Guidance on finding a mental health professional, with tips for choosing the right one.

To Cope with Life's Storms, It's crucial to have access to reliable resources for support. This appendix provides a comprehensive list of mental health resources. It includes crisis hotlines, therapy services, online support groups, and educational tools.

Crisis Hotlines and Emergency Services

- National Suicide Prevention Lifeline (U.S.): Call 1-800-273-TALK (1-800-273-8255) for free, confidential support.

- Samaritans (U.K.): Call 116 123 for crisis support and suicide prevention.

National Emergency Hotlines (Nigeria): Call 112

Lagos State Suicide Hotline-+2348058820777

Lagos State Mental Health Helpline-+234781650220

- Crisis Text Line (U.S. and Canada): Text HOME to 741741 to receive text-based crisis support.

- Emergency Services: Always dial your local emergency number for immediate help (e.g., 911 in the U.S., 112 in Europe, or 999 in the U.K.).

Professional Therapy and Counseling Services
Professional therapy and counseling can provide personalized support and guidance. Here are some recommended platforms and services:

Psychologist Today Therapist Finder

- BetterHelp: Offers online therapy services with licensed professionals, providing flexibility and confidentiality.

Extra Mental Health Resources
These resources offer a range of tools, information, and support for those seeking mental health help:

- NAMI Mental Health Support Group

- Mental Health Foundation (U.K.): Offers information on a variety of mental health topics and provides self-help resources.

- Mind (U.K.): A prominent mental health charity with resources, helplines, and community-based support.

- The Love, Peace and Mental Health Foundationan NGO based in Lagos, Nigeria.

Website: Nigerian Mental Health Coalition

Local and Community-Based Resources
Local resources can offer more personalized and community-focused support. Consider these options in your area:

Community Mental Health Centers
Mental Health Services

- Universities and Colleges: Many educational institutions have counseling centers providing support to students.

Conclusion
These resources for mental health and support offer a variety of options to meet different needs. This appendix provides a comprehensive list of services and support systems. Remember that seeking help is a sign of strength, and these resources are here to support you on your journey through life's storms. If you're facing mental health challenges, don't hesitate to reach out and find the support that works best for you.

Appendix C: Goal Setting and Tracking Templates
This appendix provides tools for goal setting and tracking progress, including:

SMART Goals Template

- Daily Planner: A customizable daily planner for managing time and tasks.

- Habit Tracker: A template for tracking habits and routines that contribute to personal growth.

SMART Goals: SMART Goals

- Action Plans: Create a step-by-step plan to achieve your goals. List the actions you need to take and set deadlines for each step.

- Progress Tracking: Keep track of your progress over time. Note what has been accomplished and any obstacles you've encountered.

Appendix D: Inspirational Quotes and Affirmations
A collection of inspirational quotes and affirmations to encourage readers, featuring:

- Quotes from Influential Figures: Uplifting quotes from well-known authors, leaders, and thinkers.

Affirmations to Help You Build Confidence
Here are some inspirational quotes and affirmations from well-known authors, leaders, and thinkers focused on the theme of overcoming life's storms:

Inspirational Quotes

1. Maya Angelou:
    "You may encounter many defeats, but you must not be defeated. In fact, it may be necessary to encounter the defeats, so you can

know who you are, what you can rise from, how you can still come out of it."

2. Harriet Tubman:
"Every great dream begins with a dreamer. Always remember, you have within you the strength, the patience, and the passion to reach for the stars to change the world."

3. Helen Keller:
"Although the world is full of suffering, it is also full of the overcoming of it."

4. Winston Churchill:
"If you're going through hell, keep going."

5. Ralph Waldo Emerson:
"Our greatest glory is not in never failing, but in rising up every time we fail."

6. Albert Einstein:
"In the middle of every difficulty lies opportunity."

7. Nelson Mandela:
"The greatest glory in living lies not in never falling, but in rising every time we fall."

8. Friedrich Nietzsche:
"That which does not kill us makes us stronger."

9. J.K. Rowling:
"Rock bottom became the solid foundation on which I rebuilt my life."

10. Desmond Tutu
"Hope is being able to see that there is light despite all of the darkness."**

Affirmations

1. "I have the strength to overcome any challenge that comes my way."

2. "Every storm I face is an opportunity for growth and self-discovery."

3. "I trust in my ability to navigate through life's difficulties."

4. "Resilience is my superpower; I rise stronger after every setback."

5. "I choose to embrace change and transform challenges into opportunities."

6. "I am capable of weathering any storm and emerging victorious."

7. "With every obstacle, I become more resilient and courageous."

8. "I release my fears and trust in the process of life."

9. "I am surrounded by support and love as I navigate this journey."

10. "I believe in my ability to overcome adversity and find peace within myself."

Conclusion
These quotes and affirmations serve as powerful reminders of the strength and resilience we possess when facing life's challenges. They can inspire us to persevere, adapt, and grow through adversity, reminding us that storms, while difficult, can lead to profound personal growth and transformation.

Appendix E: Recommended Books and Articles
A curated list of more readings to inspire and motivate, including:

- Books on Personal Growth: Recommendations for further reading on personal development and resilience.

- Articles on Overcoming Adversity: Links to articles and essays on the topic of overcoming challenges.

American Psychological Association:
"Building Resilience: Turning Challenges into Success" b

LinkedIn Pulse

Overcoming Challenges and Archiving Greatness

Both articles discuss the concept of facing adversity and growth through challenges

Self-Help and Personal Development

These resources provide tools and guidance to help you work on personal development and improve your well-being:

- Books on Personal Development:

- "The 7 Habits of Highly Effective People" by Stephen Covey: A classic book that explores habits for personal and professional success.

- "Mindset: The New Psychology of Success"* by Carol S. Dweck: Discusses the concept of fixed versus growth mindsets.

Self-Help Websites:

- PsychCentral: Offers articles and resources on various mental health topics.

- Tiny Buddha: Provides insights and advice on mindfulness, relationships, peace and personal growth.

Appendix F: Worksheets for Reflection and Growth

This appendix provides worksheets designed to help readers reflect and grow, such as:

- Reflection Worksheet: A guide for reflecting on personal experiences and lessons learned.

Strengths and Weaknesses Analysis

- Growth Plan Template : A template for creating a personal growth plan, with goals and action steps.

Reflection Worksheet

Reflection worksheets can be a powerful tool for personal growth, allowing you to process experiences, identify lessons learned, and set future goals.

Below is a guide to creating effective reflection worksheets, along with prompts and sections you can include.

Reflection Worksheet Guide

1. Title and Date

- Title:Give your reflection a title that captures the essence of the experience (e.g., "Reflecting on My Recent Challenge").

- Date:Include the date of your reflection to track your progress over time.

2. Context

- Describe the Experience:

- What happened?

- Where and when did it take place?

- Who was involved?

- **Prompt:** "Write a brief summary of the event or experience you are reflecting on."

3. Emotions and Reactions

- Identify Feelings:

- What emotions did you experience during this event?

- How did those emotions affect your behavior?

- Prompt: "List the emotions you felt and describe how they influenced your actions."

4. Lessons Learned

- Reflect on Insights:

- What did you learn about yourself?

- What did you learn about others?

- Were there any unexpected lessons?

- Prompt: "Write down the key lessons you learned from this experience."

5. Strengths and Challenges

- Identify Strengths:

- How did your strengths help you navigate this experience?

- **Recognize Challenges:**

- What challenges did you face?

- How did you cope with or overcome those challenges?

- Prompt:** "List your strengths and the challenges you encountered."

6. Future Goals and Actions

- Set Goals:

- How can you apply what you learned in future situations?

- What specific actions will you take moving forward?

- Prompt: "Write down one or two goals based on your reflections and the lessons learned."

7. Gratitude

- Express Gratitude:

- Are there people, resources, or experiences you are grateful for in this context?

- Prompt: "List three things or people you are grateful for related to this experience."

8. Additional Thoughts

- Open Space for Reflection:

- Include any other thoughts, observations, or realizations that arose during your reflection.

- Prompt:"Use this space for any additional reflections or insights."

Example Reflection Worksheet

Title:Reflection on My Recent Challenge

Date:[Insert Date]

1. Context:

- What happened?

- Where and when did it take place?

- Who was involved?

2. Emotions and Reactions:

- List of emotions:

- How they influenced my actions:

3. Lessons Learned:

- Key lessons:

4. Strengths and Challenges:

- My strengths:

- Challenges faced:

5. Future Goals and Actions:

- Goals based on reflections:

6. Gratitude:

- Three things or people I am grateful for:

7. Additional Thoughts:

- Any other reflections or insights:

Conclusion
Using reflection worksheets can helpdeepen your understanding of personal experiences and foster growth. By regularly completing these worksheets, you can track your progress, gain insights, and set actionable goals for the future. Consider making it a routine practice to reflect on different experiences, whether they are significant challenges or everyday moments.

Strengths and Weaknesses Analysis
Conducting a strengths and weaknesses analysis is an effective way to gain insight into your personal or professional capabilities. It helps you understand what you excel at and where you may need improvement.

Below is a structured approach to performing a strengths and weaknesses analysis, along with prompts to guide your reflections.

Strengths and Weaknesses Analysis Framework

1. Title and Date

- Title: Strengths and Weaknesses Analysis

- Date: [Insert Date]

2. Strengths

- Definition: Strengths are your positive attributes, skills, and capabilities that give you an advantage in various situations.

- Prompts for Reflection:

- What skills do I possess that others often compliment?

- What tasks or activities do I perform with ease or enthusiasm?

- In what areas have I received recognition or awards?

- What personal qualities do I believe contribute to my success?

- Examples of Strengths:

- Strong communication skills

- Adaptability and resilience

- Leadership and teamwork abilities

- Problem-solving skills

- Time management and organization

3. Weaknesses

- Definition: Weaknesses are areas where you may struggle or lack certain skills, which can hinder your performance or growth.

- Prompts for Reflection:

- What tasks do I find challenging or frustrating?

- Where have I received constructive criticism?

- What skills do I wish I had more proficiency in?

- What personal traits hinder my success?

- Examples of Weaknesses:

- Difficulty with public speaking

- Procrastination or poor time management

- Struggling to ask for help or delegate tasks

- Limited technical skills

- Difficulty handling criticism

4. SWOT Analysis (Optional)

- Combine Strengths and Weaknesses with Opportunities and Threats: If you want to take your analysis further, consider creating a SWOT analysis that includes:

- Opportunities: External factors that could benefit you (e.g., networking events, professional development).

- Threats: External challenges that could hinder your progress (e.g., competition, changing industry trends).

5. Action Plan

- Leverage Strengths: Identify how you can use your strengths to achieve your goals.

- Prompt: "How can I capitalize on my strengths in my personal or professional life?"

- Address Weaknesses: Develop strategies to improve upon your weaknesses.

- Prompt: "What specific actions can I take to address my weaknesses?"

- Set Goals: Create measurable goals for leveraging strengths and improving weaknesses.

- Prompt: "What are my short-term and long-term goals related to my strengths and weaknesses?"

Example Strengths and Weaknesses Analysis

Title: Strengths and Weaknesses Analysis

Date: [Insert Date]

Strengths:

1. Strong communication skills

2. Excellent problem-solving abilities

3. Adaptability in changing environments

4. Effective leadership qualities

Weaknesses:

1. Difficulty with public speaking

2. Tendency to procrastinate

3. Limited technical skills in software programs

4. Struggle to delegate tasks to others

Action Plan:

- Leverage Strengths: Use communication skills to network and build relationships in my industry.

- Address Weaknesses: Take a public speaking course and set deadlines for tasks to combat procrastination.

- Goals: Improve public speaking skills within six months and reduce procrastination by implementing a daily task list.

Conclusion
A strengths and weaknesses analysis provides valuable insights that can guide your personal and professional development. By understanding your strengths, you can leverage them to achieve your goals, and by recognizing your weaknesses, you can take proactive steps to improve. Regularly reassessing your strengths and weaknesses can help you stay aligned with your growth and aspirations. If you need further customization or specific examples, feel free to ask!

These appendices can serve as a valuable resource for readers as they navigate their journey of overcoming life's storms.

Appendix G: Relationship Building and Communication
These resources aim to help you build better relationships and improve communication skills:

- Books on Relationships:

- "The Five Love Languages" by Gary Chapman:

Explores different ways people give and receive love.

Effective Communication in High-Stakes Situations

- Relationship Counseling Services:

- Marriage and Family Therapists (MFTs): Professionals specializing in marriage and family counseling.

- The Gotten Institute: Offers resources and workshops for couples to improve relationships.

Conclusion

These extra resources cover a broad range of topics to support your journey through life's storms and beyond. Explore different resources to find the ones that resonate with you and align with your personal goals and needs.

Appendix H: Recommended References for Further Reading

Here are some recommended references for further reading on topics related to overcoming life's storms.

- "The Road Less Traveled" by M. Scott Peck:

Explores themes of personal growth and spiritual development.

- "Man's Search for Meaning" by Viktor E.:

A classic work on finding purpose and meaning through adversity.

- "The Power of Now" by Elkhart Toll: Focuses on mindfulness and living in the present moment.

- "The Resilience Factor" by Karen Reivich How to Overcome Setbacks

The book offers tools to deal with self-criticisms and negative self-images, to bear the fallout of any kind of crisis, to cope with grief and anxiety, and to boost optimism and enjoy taking risks.

These references support the key themes, strategies, and stories discussed in this Book.